ISSUES IN LAW AND MORALITY

ISSUES IN LAW
AND MORALITY

Proceedings of the
1971 Oberlin Colloquium in Philosophy

EDITED BY

Norman S. Care

AND

Thomas K. Trelogan

The Press of
Case Western Reserve University
Cleveland & London / 1973

Library of Congress Cataloging in Publication Data

Oberlin Colloquium in Philosophy, 12th, Oberlin College, 1971.
    Issues in law and morality; proceedings.

    Bibliography: p.
      1. Law and ethics—Addresses, essays, lectures.
I. Care, Norman S., ed.   II. Trelogan, Thomas K., ed.
III. Title.
LAW   340.1'12   72-86351
ISBN 0-8295-0244-0

340.1
012i

74-1868

Contents

Preface

This volume contains the proceedings of the twelfth annual Oberlin Colloquium in Philosophy (1971). The Colloquium is sponsored each year by the Department of Philosophy of Oberlin College as an opportunity for a small group of invited philosophers to present new work and to receive close discussion of it from a number of professional colleagues. In 1971 the work presented at the Colloquium fell into the general area of philosophy of law, construed as incorporating the fields of jurisprudence, political philosophy, and moral theory. While no single philosophical problem provides a common focus for all the symposia in this volume, each of them in different ways evidences a concern for questions about the justification of violations of established principles, or rules, or general human attitudes or sentiments, as these latter are involved in legal or political structures.* The severity of such violations may, of course, range in degree from broadly directed—perhaps even revolutionary—political violence, to more specifically directed disruptive behavior, to behavior which, while harmless, is yet offensive to human attitudes and sentiments. Further, it may be thought that the law itself is as capable of violations of the individual as is the individual of the law. These considerations are among the factors that complicate the task of developing a theory of justification adequate to the form of social life reflected in our legal and political institutions. We hope the symposia published here contribute to the clarification of at least some of the difficulties that reflection upon these considerations brings to light. Each symposium consists of a main paper, a set of comments, and a reply. The materials from all four symposia are published here for the first time.

* For purposes of background we provide a selected bibliography, to be found at the end of this volume, of contemporary materials relevant to these questions.

The object of the paper by Ted Honderich in the first symposium is to explore the familiar view that there is an at least very strong, if not absolutely insuperable, argument against political violence (defined, loosely, as a use of force "prohibited or not authorized . . . by a state which has authority"), together with the conviction that the argument against violence—in the case of violence to people—is "without an analogue," i.e. not open to the possibility of counter-argument invoking considerations which are similar in kind to those involved in the argument against violence. Honderich conducts his exploration through a discussion of the relevant views of two contemporary moral and political philosophers, Robert Paul Wolff and John Rawls. He argues that Wolff's view, according to which the notion of political violence is ultimately incoherent, is either wrong or uninteresting. And he argues that Rawls' form of social-contract theory, perhaps in contrast to what Rawls might contend, suggests that in certain circumstances political violence may be justified. Beyond these critiques, Honderich offers "some small beginnings" of a third view of how justification for political violence is to be appraised. Here he is concerned to urge "that questions and facts at the level of human existence take precedence over [such large ideologies as] conservatism, liberalism, radicalism, communism, generalized conceptions of the just society and the rest." His point is that while there may well be circumstances in which political violence is justified, its justification on a given occasion is not likely to be aided by recourse to philosophical theories of any great generality.

In his comments Edmund L. Pincoffs is not concerned to dispute this last point. He argues, rather, that Honderich's discussions of Wolff and Rawls need further development to be convincing, and then makes a suggestion about how the concept of violence is to be analyzed. Pincoffs notes first that "the precipitate" of Wolff's challenge to the coherency of the notion of political violence, viz. "the question of the burden of proof which must be shouldered in violating a command," is not dealt with in Honderich's discussion, and that the case against Wolff's view is thus weakened in an important respect. Pincoffs also notes that the general theory of law as of the nature of command seems uncritically presupposed by both Wolff and Honderich, though indeed recent work in the philosophy of law has made that theory very controversial; and he remarks further that such a theory is not readily made compatible with the conception of authority—by which a state has authority to the degree to which it operates according to justified principles —that Honderich opposes to Wolff's view. Finally, Pincoffs notes an obscurity in Wolff's view (one not mentioned by Honderich), namely, the difficulty of how politically normative terms such as "violence" can be said by Wolff to be meaningless, while morally normative terms such as "obligation," "right," and "wrong" are not.

Regarding Honderich's view that Rawls' theory allows the possibility of justified political violence in certain circumstances, Pincoffs argues that Honderich does not consider how, if this is the case, violence "is to be institutionalized." This last point leads Pincoffs to make a "small suggestion" concerning the justification of violence. It is that Honderich's loose definition of political violence fails to distinguish between "symbolic" and "non-symbolic" violence, with the consequence, Pincoffs claims, that "justification too easily shades off into sympathetic explanation." Pincoffs' thought is that contractees designing a society—in the sense of Rawls' theory of justice—would be more likely to "leave a place for," i.e. in some way institutionalize, symbolic than non-symbolic violence even though there can be circumstances in which the latter, as well as the former, can be justified.

In his reply to Pincoffs' several points Honderich claims, among other things, that the question of whether all laws have the character of commands is not relevant to the issue. But he makes no special objection to Pincoffs' distinction between symbolic and nonsymbolic violence.

In the second symposium the subject is disruption of legal processes, and the initial question is whether behavior which constitutes such disruption might in some circumstances be justified. Graham Hughes approaches this question by assuming a *prima facie* obligation to obey the law and then sketching two kinds of justificatory account which seem relevant to cases of disruption. One of these involves a commitment to revolution; the other involves the notion of civil disobedience. In the case of refusal to cooperate with legal procedures, an unqualified account of the latter sort hardly seems available. For on "the classical, Gandhian concept of civil disobedience" at any rate, submission to the legal system, even willingness to suffer punishment, is an integral part of the appeal to conscience that the civil disobedient wishes to make. Hughes argues, however, that a commitment to revolution is not the only justification available to those who protest the legal system. There is, he suggests, "a third position" which needs to be considered.

At the center of this third position is the view that, on the one hand, just as it is conceivable that a society might have a good judicial system and yet suffer from such basic flaws in other elements of its government that, although noncooperation with the courts would not by itself be justifiable, a general revolution would be; so, on the other hand, it is also conceivable that a society otherwise without serious flaws might have so deficient a judicial system that, although general revolution would be out of the question, noncooperation with the judicial system could be justified as a kind of civil disobedience—indeed, as "the only kind of civil disobedience that would make much sense." Hughes then enumerates a list of familiar charges (among them "selective law enforcement") against the operation of the American legal system, and points out that when groups of persons are regularly subjected to practices against which such charges are accurate they may then have persuasive moral arguments for being exempted from the "usual duties of cooperation with the processes of the legal system." Such an argument, he suggests, "underlies a good deal of radical rhetoric and especially Black Panther rhetoric."

Hughes further suggests that lawyers themselves have a special duty to bring to the attention of the relevant officials and publics the grievances of protestors, even when these do not directly concern the operations of the legal system. Indeed, indifference on the part of the legal community to legitimate grievances will only sharpen the sense of injustice in such a way as to make disruption of legal procedures more common and, in fact, to encourage a disposition to support general revolution. In sum, "a cold and cruel process of law will breed its own destroyers."

The comments by Hyman Gross are directed to Hughes' assumption of a *prima facie* moral obligation to obey the law and to certain of his claims concerning what can count toward justification of courtroom disruption. He also wishes to suggest what some proper moral grounds are for claiming that disruption is not liable to punishment or is at least open to mitigation of punishment. Gross argues both that the notion of obedience is inappropriate as a characterization of the relation between persons and the law, and that the facts and politics of actual practice do not give rise to any such general *prima facie* obligation to obey the law as would exist were there general arrangements for "mutual forbearance in the interest of the protection of all" envisioned by parties to a social contract.

These points are elucidated in such a way as to seem to us to suggest the separation of law and morality associated with legal positivism, though this is perhaps tempered by Gross's further view that policies of law enforcement are to be in accord with "an intelligent appreciation of the social evils whose curtailment is the purpose of the law." This latter view he brings to Hughes' report that the American legal system is often charged with selective law enforcement against certain groups of persons. Gross argues that "all just and prudent law enforcement is selective" and that, indeed, we can imagine a sound discretionary policy of enforcement attempting to curtail recognized social evils. But if the legal order were to conspire with malice against certain individuals, then of course "defiance of it is not only justifiable, but commendable." Gross remains, however, unpersuaded by many of the allegations of such conspiracy, and while there are indeed abuses *in* the legal system in America today, he sees no general collapse *of* the system in regard to some category of law enforcement. Finally, Gross argues that in certain circumstances—in particular, when a legal vindication of disruption is attempted and fails through morally objectionable official conduct or through lack of a real opportunity for vindication within the legal system—courtroom disruption is morally justifiable; and he finds that in other circumstances—e.g. those involving objectionable treatment during pretrial detention, worthiness of motive, or worthiness of the conduct itself—punishment for disruption should be mitigated.

In his short reply Hughes claims first that the relevance of Gross's doubts about the appropriateness of the concept of obedience to the concerns of his paper is not plain. Further, he suggests that Gross's denial of a *prima facie* obligation to obey the law rests on a consideration of the "process" by which law is made rather than the "function" of law in society, whereas the latter is the source of that obligation. Finally, Hughes notes—what he supposes Gross would agree with—that "it is clearly not the case that all selective law enforcement is just and prudent" and speculates that determining the extent to which we have a collapse *of* the legal system in some category of law enforcement might depend on a fuller discussion of what that notion of collapse is supposed to involve.

Joel Feinberg offers two main theses in the lead paper in the third symposium. He argues first that if there are private immoral acts that cause no harm, there is no justification for their suppression by the state or for their proscription by the criminal law. Second, he argues that the state is justified in preventing actions that are very offensive to others. In support of these views Feinberg identifies a set of principles which have been used in justifying certain legal restrictions upon liberty and then proceeds to assess arguments for such restrictions which make use of those principles. While "legal moralism," i.e. the principle of enforcement of morality as such, is rejected by Feinberg, he finds that the justification of liberty-limiting restrictions requires that certain basic "harm" principles be supplemented with an "offense" principle, "if we are to do justice to all of our particular intuitions in the most harmonious way."

That is, in addition to avoiding harm to persons, and avoiding harm to institutional practices and systems in the public interest, preventing offense (where offense is distinguished from harm) to others can, under certain conditions, justify legal restrictions on liberty. The notion of offense employed here is that of "offended mental states." According to Feinberg, examples of such states would include, among other things, "irritating sensations . . . unaffected disgust and acute repugnance . . . shocked moral, religious, or patriotic sensibilities, unsettling anger or irritation . . . and shameful embarrassment or invaded privacy. . . ." In his discussion Feinberg focuses on three familiar and vivid types of cases that he hopes are persuasive, namely, public displays of obscenity that are not easily avoidable, uses of speech that are abusive of or offensive to minorities, and public nudity and indecency.

An offense principle applicable to such cases must, according to Feinberg, be carefully formulated, "so as not to open the door to wholesale and intuitively unwarranted repression." The last part of Feinberg's paper is devoted to developing an adequate formulation. He argues that justificatory use of the principle of preventing offense to others must proceed under certain "mediating norms of interpretation." Among these are, first, a "standard of universality," according to which the offense cited to justify restrictions must be the reaction "that could reasonably be expected from almost any person chosen at random," rather than that of persons belonging to "some faction, clique, or party." However, Feinberg allows an exception to this norm in the case of that class of "abusive, mocking, insulting behavior" of which a typical example is that of speech insulting to members of a minority group. Here the offense principle would apply, even though the disallowed behavior might not "offend the entire population." A second norm of interpretation is "the standard of reasonable avoidability," according to which the offense principle cannot be used to justify restrictions on conduct that can without difficulty be avoided by those whom it would offend. In line with the former norm of universality, Feinberg claims that no special respect is owed to "abnormal susceptibilities" and notes that the application of both the offense principle and the principle of avoiding harm to persons requires some conception of "normalcy." A final condition of use of the offense principle is that persons whose liberty is restricted in its name "must be granted an allowable alternative outlet or mode of expression."

Michael D. Bayles introduces his comments by indicating that he disagrees more with Feinberg's approach than with his conclusions. He first notes certain troubles in Feinberg's general view of a liberty-limiting principle as a statement of a sufficient condition of justified (i.e. permissible) coercion, and then proposes an alternative account by which such a principle is construed as stating "a condition which constitutes a good reason, but neither a necessary nor sufficient one, for legislation." Further, Bayles argues that Feinberg's account has the effect of tying offense too closely to "positive morality," for it only requires that conduct "shock the sensibilities of accepted morality, religion, or politics" and places no restrictions upon the *reasonableness* of "the objects of these sensibilities as long as almost everyone has them towards the same thing." He also points out that Feinberg's paper provides no argument to show "that protection from offense justifies overriding the presumption against criminal legislation" and thus "that the evil of offensive conduct outweighs that involved in punishment."

Beyond this, Bayles challenges Feinberg's attempt to reach normative conclusions from intuitions in particular cases, claiming that "accounting for intuitions is a relevant but not conclusive consideration" in justifying adopting principles such as those under discussion in Feinberg's paper. Bayles then reviews Feinberg's examples to show that they may not necessarily lead one to adopt the offense principle. And he elaborates an alternative, "more cautious," approach to the justification of restrictions upon the conduct of persons, one that involves expanding the principle of avoiding harm to persons rather than adopting the offense principle. He notes in support of the alternative that it "does not commit one in advance to the wholesale protection of the sensibilities of a large majority without examining the merits of the particular sensibilities and their objects," and also that, for certain reasons, it does not retain Feinberg's universality restriction, though it does retain his avoidability restriction. In sum, Bayles brings against Feinberg's approach the view that the search for a clear principle to be easily applied in controversial cases "seems a hopeless task," and he claims that insofar as Feinberg is driven to the offense principle by the attempt to account for intuitions in such cases, it may be that the principle should not be accepted. Bayles prefers the alternative approach by which the concept of "interests deserving various degrees of protection" —as it is involved in the principle of avoiding harm to persons— undergoes "cautious expansion."

In his reply Feinberg acknowledges certain of Bayles' points, such as that concerning how liberty-limiting principles are to be construed, and, indeed, makes use of those points to elaborate upon parts of his main paper. For example, he discusses further how such principles specify considerations that are "always relevant or acceptable in support of proposed coercion even though in a given case they may not be conclusive," and adds remarks about the connection between his offense principle and the right of free speech, and about alternatives to the criminal law for the control of undesirable conduct. He provides "one final example"—a striking one, we venture to say—in reply to Bayles' doubts about the procedure of arguing from examples to normative conclusions. His final remarks concern how the fact of constant and rapid change in cultural standards bears upon his account, and why he is reluctant to restrict the offenses countenanced by the offense principle to "reasonable" offenses.

The final symposium begins with a paper by Gerald C. MacCallum, Jr. dealing with two questions concerning the relationship between law and action in accordance with a person's conscience. The first of these is the question of whether or not the law's demand for compliance can ever violate the conscience of an individual. In answering this question MacCallum argues that, under the common view of law as something "imposed" upon us, the law's demand for compliance "can neither violate nor threaten to violate a person's conscience," though indeed it may lead him to violate his own conscience "in a way revealing to him his failure to live up to his own aspirations for himself." MacCallum's point is that a condition of something's being able to violate a person's conscience is that it be something that person "does or fails to do," and that under the view of law in question law does not meet this condition. But MacCallum does not, for this reason, reject the common view. He argues rather that insofar as we wish to say that compliance with law can amount to or lead to violations of conscience, we must say that it does so "by leading persons to violate their own consciences in ways revealing to them that they are indeed somewhat less admirable than they had hoped to be."

This line of thought occasions a natural second question: the question, as MacCallum puts it, of "what stake we have in protecting people from such confrontations with their own shortcomings." Why, after all, should we think that persons "*merit* or *have a right to* protection against such a state of affairs"? MacCallum's interest here is in views which answer this question in terms of how punitive measures of the law constitute a danger to "the development or preservation of one's personal integrity and indeed of his status as a moral agent and even as a man." The remainder of his paper is devoted to eliciting that "vision" of what it is to be a person which underlies such views. He finds that that vision, in its emphasis on the moral autonomy of persons and on the central role of conscience in the make-up of human nature, has some features of "atomistic individualism," and that, as such, it is a "highly individualistic" and even "dominantly male-oriented" view of persons. MacCallum claims that those who argue in support of the special rights of conscience against the law do so from such a model of persons, and he ends by posing the question of whether such a model is acceptable.

In his comments Hugo Adam Bedau offers two main criticisms of MacCallum's view, and then sketches "a general position rather different from his." The first criticism is that MacCallum's account seems to preclude a use for "conscience" in the "language of judgment other than the language of self-judgment." For example, it seems to make unintelligible, or at least puzzling, what is meant by *my* claim that what *you* did weighs heavily on *my* conscience. But Bedau thinks that such discourse *is* intelligible, and that it is so because, in general, references to conscience are references to moral principles. Thus, "it is quite possible that though your acts are permitted by your principles . . . they are in violation of mine, and in this sense violate my conscience and provoke my conscientious protest of them."

Bedau's second criticism is that MacCallum's view, according to which a person whose conscience is violated fails to live up to his highest aspirations for himself, while true, is nevertheless incomplete "as an explanation of why it is wrong for a person to violate his conscience." Bedau argues that there are "other-regarding reasons" involved as well as the considerations of "moral self-regard that MacCallum stresses." Thus, "a further part of the explanation . . . is that [to violate conscience] often is to cause unjustifiable and inexcusable harm to others."

The alternative position that Bedau sketches begins with a distinction between "respecting conscience" and "appealing to conscience." It then consists of two theses: (a) that whatever is of moral worth in respecting a person's conscience "lies in the moral worth of respecting him as a person," and (b) that whatever is of moral worth in a person's appeal to his own conscience "lies in the moral worth of the principle espoused by that person." Bedau concludes by arguing in support of his identification of "consulting my principles" and "consulting my conscience," and by remarking that his view may prevent our being led, by "a due regard for the moral worth of the person" to whose conscience we make an appeal, to esteem too highly the moral worth of his conscience.

In his brief reply MacCallum focuses mainly on the first of Bedau's criticisms. He argues that one may indeed "conscientiously" protest something that another person did, but that it does not follow that what that person did is in violation of one's conscience. Thus, your acts may violate my principles, and I may protest, not because my conscience is violated, but because "I aspire to be a person who *cares* about what happens in the community": e.g. I may aspire "to take or to feel myself responsible for taking measures to see that others as well as myself act in accord with the principles and would feel remiss if I failed to take those measures." Beyond this, MacCallum notes how there is substantial agreement between Bedau and himself on other points raised in Bedau's comments. Finally, he remarks that Bedau's views about the relationship between conscience and principles are "best suited to a clearly 'secularized' conscience and thus perhaps best stated less generally than he states them."

* * * *

The members of the Department of Philosophy of Oberlin College thank the speakers and commentators for their contributions to the 1971 Oberlin Colloquium in Philosophy. Ted Honderich is from University College London (during 1970–71 he was visiting professor at Yale University and the City University of New York), and Edmund L. Pincoffs is from the University of Texas. Graham Hughes teaches at New York University School of Law, and Hyman Gross practices law in New York City. Joel Feinberg is from The Rockefeller University and Michael D. Bayles is from the University of Kentucky. Gerald C. MacCallum, Jr. teaches at the University of Wisconsin; Hugo Adam Bedau is at Tufts University. The members of the Department also thank the other invited philosophers who attended the Colloquium for their participation.

We are grateful to Oberlin College for its continuing support of the Oberlin Colloquium in Philosophy.

N.S.C. and T.K.T.
for the Department of Philosophy
Oberlin College

ISSUES IN LAW AND MORALITY

Appraisals of Political Violence

TED HONDERICH

Everyone to whom we need pay attention has the conviction about political violence in many societies that there is at least a constraining argument against it. This is so, certainly, where lives and bodies are in question. A bomb in an evacuated building usually does not, and usually should not, call up that same response. Some people are inclined, also, to the conviction that there is a fundamental argument against violence, violence to people, which is without an analogue. That is, it is of such a kind that there can be no like argument in favor of violence. My principal intention in this essay is to consider two appraisals of these convictions and then to offer some small beginnings of a third.

The convictions partly explain the linguistic fact that to allow that something is rightly named as *violence*, no matter what the higher purpose, is to allow that it is open to some moral question. While it is not inconsistent to claim moral justification for an act of violence, there is this obstacle that stands in the way to any such conclusion. The progress of the Left would be easier without it. Some apologists of political violence offer a *tu quoque* in an attempt to deal with the discomfiting fact that language does not serve their politics. They assert that the ghetto landlord also engages in violence, simply by collecting rents, that Protestant aldermen in Ulster have done so through by-laws that have kept Catholic families in degradation, that an English policeman is an agent of violence, however small his use of force. Such responses, whose morality may be superior to their formulation, have it that there is violence all about us.

There is another response to the effect that there is none. There is no violence, at any rate, of a certain important kind. We are told that in asking what can be said against political violence, conceived in a certain way, we fall into incoherence. Indeed any talk of violence, so conceived, is thought to be incoherent. The proposition, as we shall see, is bound up with the denial that there can be constraining arguments of a certain character against political violence. This appraisal, the first I shall consider, has been expressed in a number of forms. It may be profitable to examine that one which is owed to Professor Wolff.[1] It has been influential with those of a similar political persuasion.

A Right to Obedience

If this appraisal were plainly said to have the conclusion with which some of its users have credited it, that we fall into incoherence whenever we ask about violence, by way of whatever concept, we could pass on very quickly indeed. A moment's reflection on some serviceable concept, of which there are several, would lead without further ado to the truth that the appraisal was a footling one. I have in mind, for example, the conception of violence as fundamentally a use of force prohibited by law. As it happens, what we are offered is something less adventurous, if not greatly so. It is that if we fasten on *the distinctive political concept of violence*, and do such a thing as ask if violence so conceived can ever be condemned, we fall into incoherence. If we avoid incoherence by giving up that particular concept, we are thought to pay a large price.

We may begin with the claim that some kind of government or state has authority. Some kind of state, that is, has a right to be obeyed by its subjects. This claim, which needs careful handling, has been widely accepted in the history of political thought, although different kinds of state have been put forward and different arguments adduced. It is accepted today by those of us who are committed, more or less unhappily, to various states described as democratic. It has been accepted by others who have made use of the notion of a social contract, by those who have believed in a monarch's divine right, by those who have found a superiority for a class and its government in the wisdom of the class or in its historical role.

We may tentatively understand that the general claim about which there is and has been this agreement is that the subjects of at least some states are under some moral obligation to give up certain courses of action which are made illegal. There is a moral restraint or prohibition on subjects with respect to those courses of action which are prohibited by the law of the state. Subjects are in some way constrained to give up the behavior in question, despite the fact that it may be in some respect morally desirable in their view or even in some respect obligatory. This, by way of general description, is what it is for the state to have authority, to have a right to obedience. It is all very loose. The argument we are to consider will turn on more precise accounts.

Coming now to what is called the distinctive political concept of violence, it is first said to be an idea of a use of force to effect decisions against the desires of others. In these respects it is thought to be like all other concepts of violence. One might have reservations even about this much. After all, I can be violent with my own recalcitrant property, perhaps without intending to effect any decision and certainly without going against anyone else's desires. Revisions of an obvious nature are possible, however, so let us concern ourselves only with something else. The special feature of distinctively political violence is that it is a use of force either prohibited or not authorized (we are offered these different possibilities) *by a state which has authority*. It is a use of force prohibited, to remain with that, by a state whose subjects are under an obligation, some obligation or other, to obey its commands.

Let us look at a very different claim, one to which Kant gave some attention in his moral philosophy. It is that a man is under an obligation not to act in a given way unless he himself sees good reason for so doing. A part of what is meant by this is that a man is obliged not to act on the mere ground that someone has told him to do so. I do not have a reason for action in the bare fact that someone has told me to do whatever it is. With a good deal of effort, we might get something out of this, even something other than a moral truism. For a start, we should have to consider the possibility that unless we are all to become a good deal more reflective than we are, or more inactive, the range of acts in question must be limited. Humming a bit of a song while walking across a field with someone may not seem to be something that requires a good reason. At any rate, I may not have to have, in the forefront of my mind, any more than that my companion asked me to do the thing. Or, should we say that one's unconsidered recognition that a situation is inconsequential *does* provide one with a good reason for certain behavior? Again, if I lack the slightest notion of what will avert some disaster, I am permitted to do what I am told by someone who has a gleam of hope in his eye. I am under no obligation not to act. A man can fulfill his obligation and still come pretty close to doing something simply because he has been told to do it.

There is more to be said, but let us now assemble our pieces, unfinished as they are. There is an obligation not to perform many actions, or many actions in certain settings, without what seems to be a good reason. This excludes doing many things simply because one has been told to do them. Well then, no state or government can have authority, the authority that was mentioned above. That is, there is an obligation borne by every man which makes it impossible for any state to possess a certain right to a man's obedience. Or rather, to include a qualification to which we shall return, no state which is a practical possibility can ever have the right in question. It is allowed that it might be possessed by a certain ideal democratic state—ideal in that all its policies are considered and voted on by all its citizens and have their unanimous support. Such a state is a fantasy. If no state that is practically possible can have the given right to a man's obedience, however, there are consequences for the distinctive political concept of violence.

If violence is taken to be a use of force prohibited by a state with the authority in question, then there is no violence, since there is no such state to prohibit anything. No use of force falls under the distinctive political concept of violence. The concept is empty. In order to get to the further conclusion, that talk of violence of this kind is incoherent, one notices the general presupposition that the concept does distinguish between uses of force that are violent and uses of force that are not. This is a presupposition of the kind, or of one of several related kinds, present in the use of any concept. However, by the argument just given, the distinctive political concept fails to do any such distinguishing. No use of force is violent. Here we have incoherence, related to inconsistency. Given the further argument that I intend, there will be no need for greater precision on this point.

Incidentally, one can also attempt the conclusion about incoherence from the other definition of violence. There, it is a use of force not authorized, as distinct from prohibited, by a state with the right kind of authority. In this case we may try to maintain that every use of force is an instance of violence, and also the further conclusion about incoherence. Let us continue to have in mind the other form of the argument, proceeding from the definition of violence as a prohibited use of force.

What we now have is less than crystal clear. Still, it is plain enough that the argument so far does not have a merely conceptual point as its goal. That goal, rather, is a proposition of morality. The argument so far, at bottom, is something like this:

1. Each of us is obliged never to act, except perhaps in certain circumstances, on the mere ground that we have been told to do so.
2. Therefore, it is mistaken to think that any existing government could have a certain right to the obedience of its subjects.
3. One cannot claim, then, against those who do such things as set bombs, that they are violating a related obligation of obedience.

There is no reason to rewrite this latter conclusion in any less overt way. Suppose by way of analogy that one comes to believe, along with those impressed by the privacy of the soul, that it is impossible ever to assess a man's responsibility for an action. Suppose one believes, too, that it is necessary, if punishing a man is to be morally tolerable, that it be known that he was responsible for an offense. There follows the conclusion that no one ought to be punished, whatever else we ought to do about criminal behavior. The conclusion, for all that has been said so far, can be couched differently, by specifying a distinctive concept of *justified punishment*. Such punishment is of an offender of whom it is known that he was responsible for his offense. The conclusion of our bit of argument may then be that the concept of a justified punishment applies to nothing and that talk which makes use of it is incoherent.

There is, in fact, no reason to conclude this argument by somewhat Olympian observations on the concept of justified punishment. There is no more reason to conclude the other argument by talk of the distinctive political concept of violence. Some may think that this opinion can be supported by showing that neither the concept of justified punishment nor the given concept of violence is entrenched in ordinary usage or in any other relevant usage. This may be true. A better reason is that the guiding intention of both arguments is not merely to change usage—supposing that slight achievement by itself to be even conceivable—but to contribute to a change in attitude, policy, and action. Given this, what might be called the standard form for moral prescription is preferable.

What we have in the first part of the clarified argument about violence is that a man is obliged never to act, except perhaps in certain circumstances, simply because someone has told him to do so. The concern of this nostrum is clearly the moral agent or the good man. A good man is one who has the trait among others that he does not act without seeing good reason for doing so. He acts in accordance with some fact of personal responsibility, a fact which is not to be escaped and which he does not attempt to escape.

It is thought to follow from this that governments are not justified in claiming a right of obedience from their subjects. This statement, of course, like all those offered above about authority, is but a gesture. I propose that we find the particular authority that suits the argument. That is, let us see what kind of authority it is that a government cannot have if the first part of the argument is accepted. What right of obedience is it that a government cannot have if we accept that every man has an obligation not to act, anyway in most circumstances, if he does not see a good reason for doing so? What obligation of obedience is it that a man cannot have if he is under an obligation to act only for good reason?

Let us imagine a man who is wholly law-abiding and who says that he lives as he does only because the law so directs him. That is good enough for him. If we pester him a bit, he will *not* assent to various alternative arguments for his living as he does. He will not accept the account that he lives as he does because that is the lawful way *and* the law expresses his own will. Nor does it matter to him that the law expresses the will of a majority of the members of his society. He will not accept, either, that a justification of his behavior is that obedience to the law has the recommendation that it avoids greater losses, of whatever kind, than those that may be involved in disobedience. If he did assent to *any* such explanation of his conduct, he would not be the man we want, not a pure case of the obligation of the special kind that we have in mind.

We may suppose, if we want, that our man sometimes thinks there is a good reason for obeying this or that law, a reason other than that it *is* a law. At other times, he thinks there is such a reason for not obeying a law. None of this makes any difference to him. He governs his life, or the part of it with which we are concerned, by the simple principle that if something is ordered by law, he does it. He is amoral or, just conceivably, a man of one moral principle. What gives rise to action on his part is the law, and, it must be remembered, this is not to be taken as an enthymeme. It is not that obeying the law has this or that further recommendation.

It is such a man, and only such a man, who accords to his government the relevant authority or right to obedience. It is such a man, and only such a man, who accords to his government an authority that runs against the obligation of which Kant speaks. The authority in question, now that it can be seen more clearly, is an extremely curious right, not merely to behavior but to a certain genesis of behavior. It is a right to unreflective responses or, as one might fairly say, to a certain sort of person.

There remains a good deal of mystery about our man and the related authority that a government might be claimed to have. One would face great troubles in attempting to give a full characterization of what we can call the unreflectively obedient man. He may indeed be a phantasm owed to the warmth of the moral imagination. Still, it does seem impossible to argue, and not merely because of Kant's obligation, that it would be right for any government to have the authority in question. It is morally mistaken to think that any government could be justified in claiming this right of obedience from its subjects. Most important, we may grant without hesitation that there is one thing that *cannot* be said against the man who sets a bomb. It is that he has violated an obligation deriving from the government's right to his unreflective obedience.

Can this concession be expressed, even covertly, as the concession that the distinctive political concept of violence is empty and that talk which uses it is incoherent? Is there no sense in talk of a use of force prohibited by a government which has a right to unreflective obedience? Well, we can *conceive* of a government which is in fact accorded a right it ought not to have. We can conceive, further, that it puts the usual prohibitions on certain uses of force. There are more problems here. The intended substance of the argument is preserved in the overt form given above, however, so let us stick to that.

One other interim point is worth a moment. We were given to understand, before we became clearer about the authority in question, that it could be possessed by a government in an ideally democratic state. That is, subjects of that state could accord the authority to their government without infringing their Kantian obligation. This is confusion. What is true, rather, is that it is near enough a logical impossibility that the subjects of this state infringe their Kantian obligation. This is a state where all subjects consider, vote on, and in fact approve all legislation. Given that, their obedience to law cannot count as unreflective obedience. The fact that I participate in making the laws, and agree to them, does not make it morally tolerable to obey them unreflectively. On the contrary, unless I am a bizarrely divided personality, my participation makes it a logical impossibility. The confusion of thinking otherwise points to a fact to which we shall come.

We are given to understand that some large loss attaches to our giving up the specified argument against violence, which we may understand henceforth as a use of force prohibited by law. What loss is this? What do we lose if we give up the argument that to engage in violence is to offend against the state's right to unreflective obedience? The suggestion is that this is *the political argument* against violence. What can this mean? Since we are given no very explicit guidance, there must be a certain amount of conjecture in our understandings. There are at least three possibilities.

(i) Some may wonder if the argument we have is the one that can be derived from the practice of governments. Governments make laws, and these are not the giving of advice or an offering of reasons for certain conduct. Laws, it seems, are imperatives. One does not get, in a statute, a lot of reflection on why it ought to be obeyed. Hence, some may suppose, the implicit argument of governments is as follows: Do this because our enacted law demands it.

It would be jejune to allow this speculation to lead one to the conclusion that the only "politically important" concept of authority is that of a right to unreflective obedience, or to the plainer conclusion that the only "politically important" argument against violence is that it offends against an obligation of unreflective obedience. It would be as jejune as supposing that the principal argument for my repaying a loan is the single fact that on a certain day a man asks me for a sum of money.

(ii) What else is to be said? At several points in the text I am considering it to be granted that we can distinguish between right and wrong uses of force, between those that are morally justified and those that are not. We are told that there nonetheless can be no uses of force that derive from or go against authority. What appears to be suggested is that it is nonsense to talk of authority *at all* with respect to governments. It is nonsense to talk *in any way* of a government's right to obedience. It is not just that we must give up what has already been given up, authority conceived as a right to unreflective obedience.[2] We cannot condemn the man who sets a bomb as having done something prohibited by the government as a matter of right or authority, however conceived.

What lies behind this may be the supposition that to accord a right to something, or to grant authority with respect to some matter, *is* to grant an unquestionable power of decision. We are told, perhaps, that belief in *any* legitimate authority possessed by the state is the secular reincarnation of a religious superstition which has finally ceased to play a significant role in the affairs of men. To grant authority to a government *is* to grant it a right to what has been called unreflective obedience. To disallow the latter is to disallow the former.

All that needs to be pointed out here is that there is a notion of authority that is quite different, a notion that is in no way jeopardized by anything allowed so far. It is also clear. If I think there is a moral argument for complying with most of a government's commands, and I also think that there exist certain kinds of expectation or support, I may with perfect sense talk of the government's right to obedience. The expectation is on the part of the the government and society, and is an expectation of obedience to the government's commands. The support in part, is support for the government in its attempt to enforce obedience to the commands. For the government to have this right is for it to have authority, indeed authority in the most common sense.

This can be illustrated. Suppose that I am a democrat in a democracy. I do not think that *any* policy the government may pass into law ought to be complied with, but I do think, for various reasons, that some recommendation attaches to almost any policy that is passed into law, although there may be things against it. Quite often, then, I find myself in the following situation. I will vote for policy *A* over policy *B* and think it right to do so. However, if *B* wins over *A*, I will conduct myself according to *B*. Further, I will take the view that there are better reasons for complying with *B*, as a law, than *A*, supposing *A* to be against the law. Thus there is, in my view, a moral argument for obedience to almost any law. If others take this view and there exists the expectation and support mentioned above, it will be perfectly reasonable to talk of the government's right to obedience, its authority. This will be perfectly compatible with the belief that for some *A* and some *B*, there would be better reasons for complying with *A*, as a policy against the law, than *B*, supposing it to be the law.

These are perfectly ordinary conceptions of right and authority. It is clear that they need a good deal of attention, that they raise problems of several kinds. Equally clearly, we can anticipate that it in no way follows, from the fact that a government cannot have a right to unreflective obedience, that it cannot have authority at all. Most important, it does not follow that we cannot ever condemn the man who sets a bomb as having done something prohibited by the government as a matter of right or authority. What also needs to be said, of course, is that we may feel no inclination to do so, ever, even when we are totally opposed to his action. That is, we may not feel called upon to talk of authority and rights. Indeed, in serious moral inquiry, it may be thought to be talk worth avoiding. It has its temptations, as we see, and it offers no special advantage in inquiry.

(iii) There is a third hypothesis about the supposed loss we suffer when we give up the specified argument against violence. It is an hypothesis suggested by the attention that is paid, in the texts we are considering, to the history of political theory. There appears to be an assumption, unexamined and undefended, that traditional political theory has had as its principal object the establishing of a government's right to unreflective obedience. It is assumed that those who have maintained theories of a social contract, or those who have developed democratic theory, have been attempting to establish that each of a state's subjects has that obligation of obedience which is in conflict with the moral rule about having good reason for action.

It is a spectacular unlikelihood that Locke, for example, was concerned to argue for unreflective obedience. He was concerned, rather, to advance a reason for obedience. This should not be confused with anything else and, in particular, not with a reason for giving up reflection on the government's commands. It seems that Locke's contention included nothing whatever to which Kant could object. Precisely the same is true of other doctrines of authority which have places in the history of political thought. It does not matter that some of these doctrines come close to demanding absolute obedience. In fact, to suppose that the traditional political thinkers were struggling toward a proof of the rightness of unreflective obedience is to suppose them pretty well out of touch. We must see them as spending a long time giving us reasons for obeying the government, in the hope that we shall forget them.

Scholarship is not required for the main point, however. It is plain that the traditional political doctrines *can* be used in a certain way. Whatever use may have been made of them, they can be used to argue for a familiar right of a government to obedience, a right of the kind mentioned a moment ago, something to be sharply distinguished from the right to unreflective obedience. For example, there are arguments to the effect that a democratic government is superior in several respects to a dictatorship. One can proceed, in particular, toward the conclusion that there is much to be said against violence, conceived fundamentally as a use of force that has been prohibited. Let us be mindful, though, of Hume's point, that next to the ridicule of denying an evident truth is the ridicule of taking much pains to defend it.

We have been considering one appraisal of the convictions that there is a constraining argument against political violence, and possibly one which is without an analogue. Many people have supposed that some such argument is to be found in the authority of a government and, ultimately, in the reasons for that authority. The argument, we have been told, is to be put aside. It amounts to incoherence. This appraisal, for more than one reason, is mistaken. In the main it consists in the displaying of a bad argument against violence, surely an argument neither wanted nor used by anyone, and the curious assumption that other arguments which also mention authority are equally bad.

A Duty and an Obligation

Of course, we must not make it a matter of assumption that there does exist a cogent argument against violence that can be couched in terms of the authority of the state. Let us consider what is perhaps the best known of the contemporary defenses of political obligation, one advanced by Professor Rawls.[3] It is in part a residue of the traditional doctrine of social contract, and he himself has applied it to the question of civil disobedience. It offers us, as well, an appraisal of violence.

We may begin with what is now a familiar characterization of certain principles which would be realized fully in one ideal society. The first is that each member of the society has certain liberties. These include equality before the law, political liberties, and personal liberties—the latter presumably including such freedoms as those of movement and expression. Each member of the society is to have the greatest amount of such liberty as is consistent with one restraint: each other member of society is to have as much. The second principle is that economic and social inequalities are allowed only to the extent that favorable inequalities are also to the advantage of those in the society who are worst off. That is, if certain positions in society bring to their holders unequal economic and social benefits, it must also be true that the worst-off in society are still better off as a consequence. The supposition is that the society as a whole, and in particular its most impoverished part, benefits from an incentive system providing economic and social rewards for certain individuals. Without it, the worst off would be still worse off. Finally, it is a part of the second principle that the positions to which favorable economic and social inequalities attach must be open to all comers. There is equality of opportunity.

The two principles are described as principles of justice. It is not a matter of the greatest importance, but it is worth remarking that the description makes use of an enlarged although not unfamiliar conception of justice. If one understands, more strictly, that justice has to do with the equal distribution of things and with the allocating of retribution or desert, then our two principles have to do with more than justice. The first is not merely the principle that the members of the society have equal liberty, which they would have if each had half as much as was possible, but the same amount. Rather each is to have as much as he or she can, consistent with everyone else having the same. The principle appeals to a fundamental attitude that frustrations of individuals are to be reduced and, as a second priority, satisfactions increased. A lack of liberty is a frustration, its possession a satisfaction. This fundamental attitude about frustrations and satisfactions has issued in the principle of utility, although that principle is in fact an over-statement of the attitude. We are not Utilitarians, but we do share the attitude that moved Bentham and Mill. In a sentence, we temper the attitude with justice, conceived in the stricter way. The attitude, if it enters into the first of the two principles at the base of our ideal society, also enters into the second. That principle specifies that less frustration or more satisfaction may be pursued at the cost of social and economic equality.

Our first question has to do with why the members of such a society ought to obey its laws and, of course, refrain from political violence. We may take such violence to be a use of force to secure political ends, a use of force prohibited by law in the society. There is to be this obedience because members of the society have *a natural duty* to comply with all its institutions, all of which are in accord with the principles. They have a duty, as well, not to oppose the establishment of new institutions of the same character. Also, as distinct from their natural duty, they have *an obligation* that arises from the fact that they have benefitted from the institutions of their society and also from the facts that they intend to continue to do so and that they encourage others to benefit. Let us look first at the natural duty.

One might reasonably say, in explaining it, that members of the society are bound to comply with the rules of their institutions *because* the institutions are in accord with the two principles. These institutions have the recommendation that they safeguard liberty

—equal liberty—and that they secure the greatest economic and social equality consistent with the worst-off members of society being as well off as they are. These institutions, one might say, need no further recommendation. Their nature is the ground of the obligation.

We are given to understand that there is an independent argument for compliance with this society by its members. More precisely, there is an argument for the two guiding principles, and hence the nature of the society's institutions is not the only argument for complying with them. It is claimed that the two principles would be chosen by self-interested and rational men who, in a certain state of ignorance, set about deciding on principles to govern their future society. They would choose these two principles, it is said, if they were ignorant of their own natural talents and abilities, of their positions in the society to come, of the institutions of that society, and of their own future preferences, interests, and ends. Is there an additional argument here for compliance with the institutions of the imagined society? Is there an argument over and above the consideration that the society is in accord with the two seemingly estimable principles?

There would be the possibility of such an argument, although one long since defeated by Hume, if it were being supposed that there occurred acts of covenant, acts whereby the two principles were explicitly accepted.[4] This is not part of our supposition. Nor is it a part of our supposition that there occur tacit acts of acceptance, of a kind that might be thought to fit the argument. The supposition amounts only to this, that the two principles *would* be chosen by men who were self-interested, rational, and ignorant of certain things. What, then, is the independent argument? It has to do, clearly, with the nature and circumstances of the men in question. If it were suggested, for example, that certain different principles would be chosen by a collection of self-interested individuals, a majority of whom knew they would fall into a class of the strong in the society to come, as against a class of the weak, this hypothetical genesis would confer no moral recommendation on the chosen principles. Still, what virtue is conferred on our two principles if it is true that they would be chosen by individuals who *do* satisfy all the requirements? It is hard to see that any virtue is conferred on the principles by this proposition. The qualities of our choosers, of course, are not themselves moral qualities. My own inclination is to say that the proposition to the effect that the two principles would be chosen by certain men in a certain circumstance does not provide an independent argument for those principles. Nor perhaps, as is suggested to us in other places, does the proposition provide an analysis or a deeper understanding of the *principles*. The proposition is certainly not without interest, but its interest surely lies elsewhere.

If we ask why in some actual societies we do have an approach to a recognition of such principles, why we have some institutions that are partial realizations of them, the proposition enters into the explanation. It serves as a model, an idealization which has value in that in a great many actual circumstances men are in something like the position we have imagined. They cannot predict personal outcomes, and they do not wish to gamble with their lives. Even those who are in the best economic and social positions in our societies have experience of particular circumstances of ignorance. That they give some support to the two principles is to be explained, in part, by this experience. The story has a good deal more to it. It appears, however, that the proposition in question enters into an explanation of why the principles come to have a certain degree of support. It does not provide a further argument for their moral acceptability. Perhaps rather more caution is desirable. If so, we can say that any further argument that may exist has not been made perspicuous.

What we can grant, as we have, is that a member of the imagined society does have a "natural duty" to comply with its institutions and to refrain from violence. This duty rests only on the fact that the institutions are fully informed by the principles. There is also the aforementioned *obligation* that is laid on the members of our society. A man benefits from the institutions of the society, intends to continue to do so, and leads others to benefit from them. The resulting obligation, we are told, unlike the duty we have considered, arises from his own voluntary actions. These are the actions whereby benefit is procured. It is not entirely clear to me what argument is intended. Suppose a man of the imagined society does invoke the law in order to protect his own property and then breaks a law for political reasons. In so doing, he destroys the property of someone else. In what does the wrongfulness of his act consist? What is the particular wrongfulness that has to do with the fact that he himself has used the law in his own interest? It might be thought that his two acts constitute a certain particular inequality, a departure from that particular state of equality which exists in the society. But then we have nothing distinct from the duty already noticed. What he does is to disrupt a state of affairs which has a certain recommendation. We have, in his actions, an instance for the application of an argument, but not a new argument.

However, something different might be thought, namely, that the wrongfulness of the political act consists in the fact that it is not an acceptance of rightful desert. This is suggested by the emphasis on the fact that voluntary actions enter into his prior benefitting. In this reflection, we have it that by voluntarily benefitting from an institution of his society, he acquires a certain desert. We can say, more naturally, that certain behavior on his part is now owed, or called for, or fitting. This behavior is precisely other than the behavior of destroying the property of others. The issue is much more complex here, but again it can be maintained that we have nothing that is logically distinct from the duty already granted. A general analysis of desert claims suggests that they are, in the end, appeals to equality and to a principle of satisfactions and frustrations. They are this, at any rate, insofar as they constitute moral arguments rather than nonmoral responses.[5]

We emerge with the fundamental proposition that the members of the ideal society have a duty to comply with its institutions because those institutions preserve equal liberty for all and, secondly, do the best that can be done for the worst-off. That best is to be seen in terms of a level of satisfactions and also in terms of an approach to economic and social equality. There is also the point about equal opportunity. In this society, whose nature is fixed by definition, there is no possibility of an argument for illegality and in particular for civil disobedience or political violence.

If we now turn to actual societies, perhaps to those of Britain and the United States, we are invited to consider the degrees to which they give realization to the two principles. They are democracies of a kind, and they secure for their citizens something like the liberties mentioned in connection with the ideal society. They also have economies which, it is thought, go some way toward satisfying the second principle. The nature of the society, then, gives an argument for obedience, or for some obedience. We are also invited to think, again, that there is an independent argument for obedience in these societies because their political, economic, and social institutions would be chosen by self-interested and rational men in a position of ignorance, although not the same position as before.[6] Again, it appears that no independent argument exists here or, at least, that none has been made clear. We shall take it, then, in the end, that there is only the argument for obedience that is based on the nature of the institutions, the degree to which they realize the given principles. In caution, however, I shall in a moment pay some attention to the supposed independent argument.

It is plain that in our societies there are instances of disregard for the two principles. There exist privileged classes and deprived classes, and their existence cannot be justified by the principles. It can be argued that in some of these instances only violence, and not civil disobedience, can secure redress. There is a common reflection which gives some place to civil disobedience on the premise that legal protest sometimes brings a diminishing return and in the end no acceptable return. Rawls is in some agreement with this. A reflection of the same character brings together civil disobedience and violence. Sometimes civil disobedience fails. It can then be argued, in these particular circumstances, that violence is not prohibited by the two principles but rather permitted by them. It can be argued that some recommendation attaches to violence in certain circumstances, as a recommendation attaches to democracy more generally, because violence is sometimes a necessary means to equal liberty or to some level of economic and social well-being. We shall return to this.

What is also arguable, in connection with the "independent" argument, is that self-interested and rational men, in a certain position of ignorance, would choose principles of political conduct that allow for the possibility of violence. We are supposing them to have already committed themselves to the two fundamental principles and now to be engaged in a choice of subordinate principles. They may, as we have been told, opt for democracy of a kind and a certain economy. It is *as* reasonable to suppose that they will opt for the permissibility of violence in certain conceivable situations. Each of the individuals in our hypothetical assembly is self-interested and rational. None knows what position he will have in the society to come. He does not know if he will be a member of an oppressed class or an oppressing class. Each individual *does know* what it will be like to be a victim of oppression of certain kinds and in certain circumstances. In order for us to pursue adequately this speculation about a hypothetical assembly, we must have something like a decent awareness of such experiences as degradation, persecution, suffering, hopelessness, envy, and fear. We need, too, an awareness of the states of mind that follow on such experiences. We have, almost all of us, a lively response to violence and a deadened response to what calls it up. We need for our speculation, finally, an awareness of the intransigence of privilege, which, no doubt, we can come by more readily. My suggestion is that if we now endow the members of our hypothetical assembly with such awarenesses, we can conclude that the members of the assembly would give a defined place to violence in the political principles they espouse. Our speculation issues in that conclusion, at any rate, about as readily as its more comforting counterpart issues in the conclusion that the assembly would opt for a democratic system and a certain economy.[7]

In caution again, let us recall the argument that a member of the ideal society, since he has voluntarily benefitted, has a particular obligation to obey the law. I have suggested that the obligation is not logically distinct from the duty produced by the nature of the society. Perhaps, nonetheless, the obligation is a useful derivation. Let us look at its variant in actual societies and again conceive the obligation in two ways.

If one believed that a minority of one's society was being degraded, one rightly might not allow oneself to be restrained from violent political action by the fact that one had been a beneficiary oneself. Rather the contrary, perhaps. Derivations from the two fundamental principles, quite obvious ones, might rightly overcome an opposition to violence. With respect to the conception of the obligation as having to do with desert, one might rightly feel that the return which one owed was precisely not an act of further compliance with the society, but rather an act against it.

I cannot resist a further word on the smallness of the supposed obligation of obedience. Most people would not feel that a man had gone any way toward justifying the setting of a bomb if he were able to establish that he had eschewed, as far as he could, the benefits offered to him by society. He would not do himself much good, either with his supporters or his detractors, by pointing out that he had not called the police when his house was broken into. The smallness of the argument in this case is one with the smallness of the argument in the other case, where a man benefits from his society before destroying the property of someone else.

To return to the principal argument, and my reply, the argument is that British and American societies are such that there exists a duty of obedience to law and in particular a moral prohibition on political violence. The strength of this argument depends in part on the extent to which these societies realize the two fundamental principles. The second of these was that economic and social inequalities are justified only if any reduction in them would also reduce the benefits of those who are worst off. In this connection it is admitted that it may seem likely that those at the top could be brought into something much more like a state of equality with those at the bottom, without the latter being still worse off. It may seem likely, that is, that incentive in our societies could be preserved without the gap between the rich and the poorest being so great.[8] At this point an additional economic consideration is introduced.

It is that the production of goods depends not only on an incentive system, but on something that in our societies is closely connected with it, real capital accumulation. What we are to understand is that we could, for one or perhaps a few generations, reduce the gap between rich and poor, by reducing benefits to the rich, and that we would not pay the price of reducing the state of life of the poorest. However, this would have the effect of reducing real capital accumulation and so, in the end, the effect of depriving future generations of the poorest of the degree of well-being that might otherwise have been theirs. I have stated the argument briefly but not, I hope, unfairly. One reply, which seems obvious, is that there is but a contingent connection between real capital accumulation and the existence, as we know it, of extreme economic and social inequality. One can hardly ignore the fact that there exist different economies which satisfy an analogous requirement of real capital accumulation and do not do so by lodging the capital with a class of overwhelming privilege. There seems no quick or slow argument to the conclusion that a society must do its saving by sustaining the existence of great inequalities. We need not dismay ourselves by the reflection that the economic theory in question is extensive and unsettled. We can rest on the fact that there do exist economies which face futures as secure as those of America and Britain and do not sustain similar systems of inequality.

If it can be argued, at greater length than Rawls allows himself, that other virtues attach to lodging real capital accumulation with a class of privilege, there is a further reply. Privileged classes, very generally, come to possess greater wealth and benefit than any economic or political argument can require. If they defend their position of overwhelmingly favorable inequality with intransigence, then there is the possibility of violence justified by the two principles.

What we have, then, is an indication of the failure of a strategy. Its intention was to show that our societies make some tolerable approach to the realization of the second principle. On the contrary, it can be maintained that there is no barrier of the given kind in the way of greatly reducing economic and social inequality while maintaining the standard of those who are worst off. A man need not accept that his state is forced upon him by the fact that the most efficient steps are being taken to bring him into greater equality. There is not *this* obstruction in the way to the conclusion that political violence is permissible. The two principles, in particular circumstances, may point *toward* rather than away from violence.

There are, I think, many other replies to the essential supposition that our societies are faced with hard and restraining facts, and so must be regarded as making a tolerable movement toward a more satisfactory realization of the two principles. For reasons to which I shall come in a moment, I shall not consider these replies. Rather, let us notice that there are also difficulties of another and equally fundamental kind. A man can feel that social advance is too slow, and he can also feel that it is not advance in the right direction. That is, the two principles indicating that direction can hardly be regarded as sacrosanct. Certainly it would be absurd to dismiss them as constituting other than a careful and well-judged moral position. There can be no doubt, I think, that they are superior to what is conceived as their principal competitor, the principle of utility. They are superior, as I have suggested, because they take into themselves the attitudinal foundation of the principle of utility and also because they avoid the excess of that principle.

They differ from the principle of utility, further, in that they contribute to a lower level of theory. They have the role that in Mill's moral and political philosophy is shared by two generalizations, the principle of utility and its unhappy derivation, the principle of state intervention. For several reasons, there is no easy pairing possible, but the first of our two principles is most akin to Mill's rule about intervention in the lives of individuals. Let us consider the first principle for a moment. Our societies are to accord as much liberty to all as is consistent with each member having the same amount. Two further things are said about it, the first being that an attempt must be made to decrease those accumulations of wealth that enable individuals to make unfair use of their liberty. We must move toward a position where there is not merely equality before the law, but an equal capability of making use of that equality. This is, of course, estimable. It is the second thing which is open to objection: that the liberty principle must place a restraint on our attempts to raise the level of the worst off in society.[9] This, of course, is absolutely distinct from the supposed restraint placed on our attempts by the necessity of capital accumulation. What we have is the claim that there is a prohibition on any infringement of liberty, even though it might serve to raise the level of the lowest class in society. There is this prohibition at any stage of social progress.

It is hard to estimate what is in question here, since it is not absolutely clear what liberties we are to have in mind. Furthermore, Rawls allows for what would be regarded by some as incursions on a liberty, the liberty of possession of property. Still, it seems probable that what we are intended to accept is that some core of liberty is to be protected against any infringement, even if this would be in the interest of improving the lot of the wretched in society. It is hard to see that there can be *no* stage of social progress in which such an infringement could be justified. It is hard to see, if one takes the comprehensive view of society toward which we are urged, that there is some distinction of absolute moral importance between depriving a man of his greater capability to make use of liberties and taking such steps as would reduce liberty. One can take the view, indeed, although the matter is bedevilled by the want of a clear definition of liberty, that such past social progress as is now approved by all depended upon infringements of liberty.

This is one of several similar objections that a man can have, not to the rate of social advance but to the principles which are to govern that advance. There is also something else. Fundamental principles are propositions of a certain character. The same thought, in a certain sense, can have different attitudinal embodiments. There are no neat, direct, and indubitable deductions of any practical value to be made from fundamental principles. What one gets from a principle is a function not only of what it says but also of how it says it, a function not only of what it says but also of its informing spirit. The second of the two principles urged upon us is that only those social and economic inequalities are to be allowed which are essential to the worst-off in society having as much well-being, if that is what it is, as they have. The principle incorporates, overtly, the attitude that for some foreseeable future, we must tolerate very considerable and, indeed, gross inequalities. The attitude is defended as deriving from a sense of reality, a grasp of those hard facts of life to which we are so often directed.

Of course, the principle might be put, and used, rather differently. It carries the thought that a truly satisfactory society is one in which all members enjoy a high and *equal* standard of well-being. This is, indeed, the foundation of its virtue. Why not have a more consonant expression of it? Why not give it a more fitting character? A man whose life is such that if it were visited on other members of society, they would endure it as a horror, might reasonably feel more restraint if he could believe that his society were informed not merely by tolerable principles, but by tolerable principles of urgency.

We have been considering doctrines that bear on the convictions that there is a coercive argument against political violence and an argument against it that is different in kind from any argument for it. We considered and rejected an appraisal of these convictions having to do with what was called an incoherence. There is no general barrier in the way of certain arguments to the effect that we have an obligation to keep the law. We have latterly been considering another appraisal of our convictions. Here, despite what has been said, our conclusions must be tentative. What has emerged, I think, is that there is an argument of some strength for obedience to law, but one to which replies of several kinds are possible. There is no likelihood of a fundamental argument, as some have supposed, that is without analogues. Those values which enter into argument against violence can enter as readily into an attempt to justify it. If there is an independent argument for obedience, having to do with a hypothetical contract, there is a related argument for violence in defined situations.

Another Beginning

These latter conclusions, having to do with the second appraisal, are tentative for good reason. The offered appraisal of political obligation, and my criticisms of it, are well above the fray. I do not mean to suggest only that we must have propositions of great particularity in order to draw conclusions about actual historical situations. That much is obvious. What is less obvious, perhaps, is that solutions to a considerable number of problems at a lower level of theory are required if we are to have anything like an adequate view of the justifications, perhaps the obligations, of obedience and disobedience. To return to Mill for a moment, if he fails to produce a useful principle of state intervention, he does nonetheless offer considerations of great value in *On Liberty*. There is, for example, his discussion of the problem of freedom of opinion. What we require, with particular relevance to violence, are certain answers at about that level of reflection. These are fundamental. We require them for a developed theory, including its first principles. These latter can only be summations.

1.   One's fundamental opposition to violence, to begin with that, rests on the facts that people are killed, maimed, injured, made to suffer. It rests, not much less, on the consequence that others related to them are made to suffer. No morality worth a moment's hesitation can give easy accommodation to these facts. Any morality which rides over them discredits itself, as does any quickly excusing theory of historical inevitability. Nonetheless, there are other failings. One of them has to do with a reluctance actually to

understand those circumstances which may be expected to persist in the absence of violence. There can be no doubt here, or generally, of the necessity to morality of empathetic understanding. It is something that typically is avoided, out of more motivations than crass self-interest. The question of whether or not violence will put an end to the circumstances which call it up, as well as the question of whether it alone can end them, will get some attention in a moment.

It seems in no way rhetorical to observe, as I have, that some large minority of members of our societies, if their lives were altered in a certain way, would experience them as lives of horror. I have in mind an alteration such that their new existence would be that which now *is* the lot of another minority. If one brings to mind, and not for a passing moment, what touches one most closely, perhaps one's children and their situation, it must be impossible to think of tolerating certain transformations. Our children might go to those schools that make our commitment to equal opportunity no more than hypocrisy. It is probable that they would, as do some children, not merely be savaged, but become savage. Their resulting culture would be one of aggression.

Shall we say that such a prospect, if there were a threat of its realization, would carry a distress for us wholly unlike the distress that it has for those for whom it *is* the future? No doubt this is in some degree true. Distress in some part is a consequence of prior expectation. It is also true to a degree that the destructive circumstances themselves, as against the contemplation of them, will have a lesser effect on those who have not anticipated something else. For such reasons there once was, whether in terms of equality or in terms of satisfaction and frustration, *an* argument for the institution of slavery. Neither the bare lack of such goods as freedom and property, nor equality of these goods, is of fundamental importance. What is important is avoidance of the experience of distress, and it may be avoided despite the absence of certain goods. Similarly, what is important is equality of experience, which might obtain despite inequality of goods. It may be, despite these facts, that there existed a higher reason against slavery. What is certain, in connection with more fundamental moral reflections, is that the argument of different expectations is a vanishing one. Each slave class took up, to an increasing extent, the expectations of its masters. Today, oppressed classes in our societies are as aware of their situation as is needed for fundamental moral argument. That their awareness is not yet ours does not make it reasonable to continue to weigh the goods of the world in two sets of scales.

There is, of course, a tradition of sensitivity, well protected by philosophical moralists, which is against the consideration of appalling problems. We are, with decent men, to recoil from a balancing, a calculation, which has in it a man's life or his limbs. Unless we can assume the saving grace of a just war, which all sides do, we are not to be open to reflection on the possibility that a violent death can be compared with a thousand lives of degradation. We may give up the tradition. It is not that staying within the tradition allows us to avoid giving answers to questions. We give answers, all right, and act on them, but without paying the price of reflection.

If the social emotions of whole classes of individuals have resentment and hostility, or indeed hatred, as their substance, how does that stand to the injury of a policeman? If the probability of adequate medical treatment for fatal or crippling disease is a function of money, what comparison shall we make with attacks on soldiers or the inadvertent killing of children? If by far the greatest part of a society's wealth is in the control of a very few, if privilege and traditional power of every kind come close to being their possession, how does this stand to a number of deaths by violence, fewer than those caused by criminal negligence in industry? If there is that distance, seen by all, between rotten ghettos and middle-class lawns, how does that stand to rioting and looting? Do we, more generally, feel too much about violent death, or feel about it in the wrong way, given those other kinds of experience which last a lifetime and are also unspeakable?

We share a determination not only to stand away from such questions, but to approach them, if we do, shielded by bits of worn doctrine, social perspectives, self-serving economics, and large ideologies. No one can look at these questions with the eye of an innocent. Any demand of this character would be pointless. One can demand, however, that questions and facts at the level of human existence take precedence over conservatism, liberalism, radicalism, communism, generalized conceptions of the just society, and the rest. That this demand is falsely made in our societies, and falsely met, is a familiarity. A proof, I take it, is to be found in inaction.

By way of parenthesis, let us notice that we should not be surprised that the Left has resort to *tu quoque* argument, which at best may be a tolerable appeal to a rule of equality. It is no surprise that we are told that policies of victimization and repression, which are not and do not include uses of force, are acts of violence. It is no surprise either that Wolff should attempt to make *tu quoque* argument by the Left unnecessary, by attempting to deprive the opponents of violence of their special accusation. Opposition to these several enterprises of the Left need not come out of a pedant's concern for correct usage. It may come from a conviction of the social importance of truth. It may come from an unwillingness to allow certain easy victories to those who are opposed to radical change. To tell a man that an iniquitous housing policy is an act of violence is to enable him, by way of his correct reply that it is not, to avoid facts of an incalculably greater moral importance. There are, of course, perfectly correct replies-in-kind to condemnations of some political violence. The American army in Vietnam has engaged in barbarous violence, uses of force that offend against primary principles of humanity. We have been primarily concerned, as we shall be, with violent protest against things other than war.

2.   It seems apparent, then, that any truly adequate appraisal of violence must begin at that level of reflection where one encounters problems of the kinds mentioned above. It is mistaken to think that one can begin anywhere else, with rational hope. Perhaps, however, in some circumstances, rational hope is something that we cannot have. Even those complexities that have to do with individual experience are immense.

Are there killings that no careful man can judge to be justified or unjustified? What are we to say, even now, when many of the returns are in, about deaths which have occurred in those revolutions and uprisings whose legacy has come to be generally accepted, indeed to be celebrated? If there is this ignorance as to circumstances in our own time, what are we to do? It seems a fact that there are occasions when judgments of a moral character are no more than deliverances of habit and can be no more than that. Perhaps our obligation, one we can fulfill, is to seek to ensure that such moral problems do not arise. It appears that the only way we can do so is to secure radical social and economic change. To suppress unlawful action instead would not be a way of avoiding the problem of its justification.

We may be told, of course, that in circumstances of ignorance there is an irrefutable obligation to refrain from violence. How does that come about? It is not as if the choices we are considering are between acts of violence and nothing much. To think that circumstances of ignorance give one *any* answer to what may or may not be done is to misunderstand the contention absolutely. A circumstance of ignorance is one where *no* rational choice of evils can be made. To suppose that there is an irrefutable obligation is to suppose that the circumstance is not one of ignorance. To confuse the argument so quickly would be to give evidence of precisely that reluctance to enter into reflection which has been identified.

There is a related point. It is often said, when it is thought that there *is* some possibility of rational decision, that what is in question is harm that is certain, to a victim of violence, and the uncertain prospect of good. What is to be noticed here of relevance to our present reflection, which has to do with the character of experiences and not their probability, is again the likelihood of a reluctance to consider the issue. The situation may be more perspicuously described in terms of harm and the ending of harm. The man who has violence in mind need not be contemplating the causing of distress in order to secure the gaining of satisfactions, but the causing of some distress to secure the ending of other distress.

In all of this little has been said about damage to property in order that we may face directly the principal challenge to violence and also for the reason that the problem of property-damage is more tractable. This is so, certainly, when the damage is to public property and also when the damage is to private property the destruction of which does not bear on individuals in certain ways and does bring compensation. Beyond doubt, those who believe themselves called upon to perform acts of violence must have much greater reason for violence to persons and for violence which carries that possibility. The restraints are not of that order when what is destroyed is an empty pub or indeed a Congressional washroom.

3. There are other whole categories of questions which stand in the way of any adequate appraisal of political violence. One, which is also a matter of unreflective assumption, has to do with the effectiveness of violence. It is remarkably easy, as essays in philosophical journals attest, to avoid moral difficulty by the presumption that violence does not work, that it solves nothing. This generalization, in the face of history, is a nonsense. That there is the large question of when it works, the question of what conditions must obtain, is a truism. Perhaps the question is best approached through another one, that of *how* it works when it does. Violence, usually, does not have deterrence as its principal function. Deterrent violence must be an effective coercion of government and classes, more particularly a direct threat of such a size that it stands in analogy with the coercion of an individual by punishment or its threat. Thus, the deterring of governments and classes from certain courses of action, by violence, is a likelihood only when violence rises to the level of revolution or civil war.

If political violence in our societies is seen, as commonly it is, as an attempt at deterrence, it is reasonable to suppose that it will not succeed. There is the problem, certainly, of explaining its success in the past. Political violence typically has another function. As I have said, we are familiar with circumstances in which a succession of nonviolent attempts to change society ends in small amelioration. Ordinary political activity, in this sequence, is followed by increasing civil disobedience. Violence, the successor, may have precisely the same goal as its predecessors. It may have, and achieve, the goal of establishing for a society the reality of wants and needs of a minority, the centrality and the intensity of those wants and needs. There is a smaller but related truth about the effects of political violence on the self-awareness of the oppressed.

Acts of outrage, seen in this way, are an extraordinary part of the political process. I have in mind a process in which conflicting wants and needs come to be comprehended and an accommodation reached. This is to be distinguished from a process in which one side, by force or its threat, actually exerts its will over the other. Given this general conception of how it may come about that violence is effective, it becomes less difficult to arrive at some conclusion about its effectiveness.

4.   There is, inevitably, vastly more to be considered. I shall end, nonetheless, with a comment on one related problem. It is also inevitable, and rightly so, that it will be argued that even if violence would sometimes be effective, it is to be avoided in favor of slower social progress of a nonviolent nature. Change will come without violence, and violence is therefore beyond justification. One reply is obvious. Even if we grant that this change will come, there is at least the problem of *when* it will come.

We are enjoined to save, by capital accumulation, for future generations. Are men also to find an acceptance of *their* present distress in a contemplation of the possible lives of others, perhaps their children? It seems, rather, that weight must be given to a demand for change now, change within a man's lifetime. What more relevant time-span is one to take into account? It is not as if it were a physical impossibility to change our societies fundamentally within the span of a man's life. There have been related changes in a lifetime, and they have been secured without appalling cost. It has been said before, and it is worth repeating, that we become the prisoners of the present and of a place. Things other than the *status quo*, and limited departures from it, are possible. It is therefore not unreasonable for a man to take a thin satisfaction from the promise of what he will never experience. It may be reasonable for him not to be restrained by those who would have him act differently, if acting in those ways would not change his only life.

5. I do not pretend to have done much more than raise these several issues. My principal point is that they and many others remain before us and that no satisfactory appraisal of violence is possible without a true inquiry into them.

NOTES

1. Robert Paul Wolff, "On Violence," *Journal of Philosophy* 66 (1969) : 601–16; *In Defence of Anarchism* (New York: Harper and Row, 1970).

2. "Men everywhere are prone to certain beliefs about the legitimacy of political authority, even though their beliefs are as groundless as metaphysical speculations. The most sophisticated of men persist in supposing that some valid distinction can be made between legitimate and illegitimate commands. . . ." ("On Violence," p. 602).

3. John Rawls, "Justice as Fairness," in *Philosophy, Politics and Society*, Third Series, ed. Peter Laslett and W. G. Runciman (Oxford: Blackwell, 1962), pp. 132–57; "Distributive Justice," in *Philosophy, Politics and Society*, Third Series, ed. Laslett and Runciman (Oxford: Blackwell, 1969), pp. 58–82; "The Justification of Civil Disobedience," in *Civil Disobedience: Theory and Practice*, ed. Hugo Adam Bedau (New York: Pegasus, 1969), pp. 240–55.

4. David Hume, "Of the Original Contract," in *Essays and Treatises on Several Subjects* (Dublin: 1779), reprinted in *Political Man and Social Man*, ed. Robert Paul Wolff (New York: Random House, 1966), pp. 83–99.

5. Ted Honderich, *Punishment: the Supposed Justifications* (Harmondsworth: Pelican, 1971).

6. The assembly has chosen its two first principles in the state of ignorance sketched before. Now it chooses a constitution and an economy, roughly speaking, knowing certain general facts about the society to come, notably facts about its economic possibilities. Members of the assembly do not know what positions they will have in the society to come. ("The Justification of Civil Disobedience," p. 244.)

7. The foregoing reflections, obviously, can be widened in other ways that I have not considered, so as to bring them into touch with certain contemporary realities. A national society can fail in its responsibilities to people other than its own members. It can depart so far from justice in its dealings with other societies that it makes possible an argument for internal political disobedience and, in certain circumstances, political violence. Here, if anywhere, there is the possibility of what we have been calling an independent argument. Our imagined assembly of individuals, those who judge and choose, will be larger than before.

8. Rawls, to his credit, despite the consideration to which I am coming, does not join forces with those defenders of incentive who seem able to sustain belief in the necessity of precisely the inequalities that mark our societies today. To believe this is to believe that if one man is to have *even* the filthy room he has, indecent food, some drink, and a television set, it must be that another man has a scattering of homes and cars, an airplane, and about as many as he happens to desire of whatever material goods can be brought to mind.

9. See, for example, "Distributive Justice," p. 72. I take it that this is a second thought on the part of Professor Rawls. Cf. "Justice as Fairness," p. 134.

Comments: Honderich on Violence

EDMUND L. PINCOFFS

Ted Honderich's concern is with analyses of political violence which, so he contends, prevent or bypass full discussion of the question whether political violence is ever justified. Robert Paul Wolff holds that the question of justification cannot be raised because the very notion of political violence is incoherent; John Rawls' analysis of justice makes it seem difficult if not impossible ever to justify violence. But, contends Honderich, Wolff has failed to show the incoherence of the notion of violence, and Rawls' analysis can be shown to warrant convincing arguments for violence, given a ghetto-perspective of his principles of justice. Arguments for violence must, on Honderich's view, be taken more seriously than they can be taken on either Wolff's or Rawls' view. In these brief comments I will not challenge Honderich's overall conclusion that serious attention to arguments in favor of violence is indeed called for; but I will suggest that his analyses of Wolff and Rawls themselves need more discussion. In closing I will offer a suggestion about the analysis of violence.

I

Wolff's argument, if I may in light of Honderich's careful presentation abbreviate it, is that it makes no clear sense to speak of the justification of political violence because political violence must be understood as violence against morally justified authority. But the notion of morally justified authority can be seen to be incoherent when we reflect on the demand of moral autonomy that we act only on reasons which we ourselves can accept as good. Thus, that a given act has been commanded by an authority, by a duly authorized government, is not in itself a reason for compliance. As autonomous moral agents we will comply only if we think there is good reason to do the act. But if the notion of morally justified political authority is incoherent, then the notion of violent action against that supposed authority is incoherent too, and the question when political violence is justified cannot arise. Honderich's reply is, essentially, that it is only by reference to an unacceptable notion of political authority—one which demands unreflective obedience to the state—that political authority turns out to be, if not incoherent, at least morally unacceptable. But, since no one in his senses, or with his wits about him, thinks that this is what political authority requires, the argument falls to the ground. What political authority demands is not unreflective but reflective obedience. Once this is recognized, the question is rehabilitated, and we can once again ask what the principles are upon which political violence may be justified, if ever it can be. Wolff's talk, then, about "incoherence" and "conceptual emptiness" adds nothing to his argument. He is offering a moral prescription, that we should never obey a command merely because it is a command, no matter whose command it is. But having accepted this prescription, we would still, Honderich argues, have to ask when the commands issued by political authority should be obeyed, since these commands are not mere military barks but are injunctions addressed to thinking subjects. They do not command obedience merely on the ground that they have been issued, but they claim rationality and applicability to the situation in which the subject may find himself.

If this is, as I hope, a fair brief summary, I find myself not altogether satisfied, first because I suspect that there does remain a difficulty, which Wolff could have formulated more precisely, and second because the whole discussion between Wolff and Honderich presupposes a theory of the nature of law which is not self-evidently true, the theory that law is a kind of command.

Suppose it be granted that as an autonomous moral being I must act only on reasons that I myself accept as good. Then it would follow that I must do those things which, whether I am commanded to do them or not, I have good reasons for doing. Suppose also that it is reflective obedience which is expected of me. Is there no longer any tension between the demands of autonomy and the demands of obedience? If reflective obedience is demanded, still it is obedience which is demanded. But why should I obey? Why should I give any more weight to the commands of the government than I do to my own reasons? Why should I give any weight to any commands at all? But what is the very least that political authority can demand of reflective subjects? I suppose it must be that they impose upon their moral reasoning a minimal restriction: that if they disobey the commands of the government then the burden of proof is upon them to show that they are morally justified in doing so. But why, as a Wolffian autonomist, should I accept this burden? It does set limits on my autonomy. It does make it necessary to take into account what I may think there is no good reason to take into account, that the act has been commanded. Wolff's argument may not be sound, as I think it is not; but its unsoundness will not be shown merely by reminding him that what is commanded is reflective rather than unreflective obedience. As a matter of fact, it is at least open to question whether a government may not, with respect to certain exigencies, be morally justified in demanding unreflective obedience. At any rate, the question of the burden of proof which must be shouldered in violating a command is the precipitate of Wolff's challenge, and we have not been shown how it is to be washed away by allowing that political obedience may be reflective.

My second doubt concerns the need to adopt a command theory of law as the background for a discussion of political obligation. Honderich does not challenge Wolff's identification of law with command, but I think that he should. The theory is itself notoriously full of difficulties. If a law is a command, whose command is it? Attempts to specify seem only to blur the line between legislation and administration of the law. Lots of laws do not look like commands at all, including all of those rules that Hart denominates "secondary"—rules of recognition, change, and adjudication. To think of law as command is to think of failure to conform to the law as disobedience to him who commands. It is to introduce a paternal or feudal background into the discussion of legal obligations which is not easily reconciled with the conception of authority that Honderich opposes to Wolff's. It is not, Honderich rightly wants to insist, simple obedience to a sovereign which is in question, but to an authority that rests on rules, the justification of those rules, and the justification that can be given for having a system of rules by which to be governed.

In addition to these doubts about Honderich's assessment of Wolff's argument, I find that there is another strand of argument in Wolff which Honderich might consider, since it seems to lend independent support to Wolff's contention that the justification of violence cannot be meaningfully discussed. Wolff mentions, as one of three propositions he sets out to prove, that "The dispute over violence and nonviolence in contemporary America is ideological rhetoric designed to bring about certain political ends."[1] He also argues that "the concept of violence serves as a rhetorical device for proscribing those political uses of force which one considers inimical to one's central interests. Since different social groups have different central interests . . . it follows that there are conflicting definitions of violence."[2] The conflicting definitions are, then, but persuasive definitions; and there is no rational ground for choice between them, since they are literally meaningless. But if this is so, then again the question of the justification of political violence will be logically impossible to answer.

The difficulty for Wolff in this line of argument is that he must show how it can apply against politically normative terms like "violence" but not at the same time against morally normative ones like "obligation" and "right" and "wrong." For even though he is a political skeptic he is not a moral one. His argument assumes that we are not engaging in mere rhetoric when we call some actions right and others wrong, that our autonomy consists precisely in our legislating these matters for ourselves.

In conclusion, if Wolff's argument fails, Honderich has not shown that it has done so. **(A)** He has not recognized that if there is a burden one must shoulder in violating the law, then to that extent one cannot act for any reason which seems to him good, so that the tension between autonomy so defined and the duty to be law-abiding is not released by noting that no government has a right to unreflective obedience. The question is still open whether autonomy is not limited by the *prima facie* rightness of obedience to the state. (B) Honderich follows Wolff in assuming a command theory of law which works in Wolff's favor if the point that must be made against him is that political authority itself rests upon, or can rest upon, rationally defensible grounds. (C) Honderich has not taken into consideration an independent non-cognitivist argument intended to establish the incoherence of the concept of political violence.

II

Honderich's criticism of Rawls is a more subtle one, and I find that I am in agreement with much of what he says. The general objection is that Rawls' case for political obligation is presented in such a way as to lead us not to take seriously enough a hard decision which must sometimes be made: to employ violence in the interest of alleviating intolerable suffering and degradation. The analysis falls into two parts, corresponding first to what Honderich believes to be an independent argument for Rawls' two principles of justice and second to the moral acceptability of the principles themselves.

The independent argument is that self-interested men in the original position, ignorant of any factor which could tip them off to their fate under the principles chosen, would naturally choose the two principles for the adjudication of complaints against the going practices of a society. I will, for the purposes of this paper, leave aside the question of whether Rawls intends this delineation of the original position to count as an argument for the principles,[3] and will focus instead on what I take to be Honderich's chief concern. It is that in deciding what principles to accept, and what constitution, there seems to be no good reason to suppose that Rawls' men would not naturally want to leave a place for violence as a last resort.

It should be noted in passing that Rawls does not in fact rule out violence as a last resort. In "The Justification of Civil Disobedience," he says that "by taking part in civilly disobedient acts one does not foreswear indefinitely the idea of forceful resistance . . . which may conceivably be justified 'even in a democratic regime."[4] Even so, it may be questioned whether Rawls' analysis does not lead him to underplay violence as a serious option. Honderich is inclined to think that it does. I am inclined to think that if Rawls does not treat violence at length, it may be because as a matter of judgment he does not believe that it is likely to be justified in the actual British and American societies which are foremost in his thoughts. The topic of the extent to which the Rawlsian analysis admits of the justification of violence is nevertheless well worth pursuing, as Honderich insists it should be. Honderich suggests that it does in two different ways, corresponding to two different stages of the proceedings which Rawls imagines: first of all in the original position and secondly in an already constituted society.

In the original position, Honderich thinks, it is at least arguable that men would choose principles which would allow for the possibility of violence. They would likely do this, he believes, if they have a lively awareness not just of the evils of violence, but of the conditions that sometimes drive men to violence: "degradation, persecution, suffering, hopelessness, envy, and fear" and of the "intransigence of privilege" which can lock the worst off beyond hope into their miserable lives. In an already going society, of course, we may stray very far from the principles of justice in the way in which our institutions are designed, but we are even more likely to do so in the way in which they are administered. These are points which could be expanded persuasively, but perhaps it is unnecessary to do so here. It seems that in general the sort of restriction that Rawls' men try to avoid is institutional arrangements that do not give them an equal chance in a general competition. But it may fairly be asked how much the loser in such a competition is to lose. Is it merely that he does not get as far or as much as the winner, or is it something much worse than that: a life for him and his children of horror and brutality? If this is to be a possible inescapable outcome, under the rules, then what is the self-interested and ignorant man in the original position to say to that? Or what is the man to say who has, in a going society, exhausted every recourse, including civil disobedience, to escape such a life? Honderich presses such questions ably and justifiably against Rawls. But I do not think that, in the space he allows himself, he faces up to the problem how, if violence is to be allowed in such extreme circumstances, it is to be institutionalized. That is, we must face up to the question, in Rawls' terms, of what provisions we are to offer in a constitution which would satisfy the man in the original position who is fearful of the fate he may suffer. Are we to offer him a general dispensation which allows him, when he cannot obtain legal satisfaction, to resort to violence? The difficulty with this, of course, is that he would by hypothesis have to offer the same dispensation to everyone else. But surely this general dispensation would give him pause. It would be open to self-serving interpretations, which by hypothesis can undergo no public process of scrutiny, and would consequently be likely to generate a dangerous and unstable social order.

In his essay on civil disobedience, Rawls comes closest to a discussion of the justification of violence. Here it is apparent that Rawls regards it as a virtue of civil disobedience that, unlike violence, it admits of action which, while illegal, is principled and is in fact best understood as an appeal to just those principles of justice that everyone acknowledges against the abuses of the system which is supposed to honor those principles. Violence, on the other hand, is by implication unprincipled or, at any rate, likely to be so. This leads me to a small suggestion concerning the justification of violence, with which I will close these comments.

III

Violence is thought of by Honderich as "a use of force to secure political ends, a use of force prohibited by law in the society." This is, as he recognizes, a rough-and-ready definition. It makes no claim to completeness. Even so, it is worth mentioning that it misses making a distinction which could be helpful in distinguishing justified from unjustified violence. To make the distinction, we must draw a rough division-line between violence that is symbolic in intent and violence that is not. Symbolic violence may, like nonviolent civil disobedience, serve as an appeal to the majority's sense of justice. It is an act designed to call attention to a state of affairs which should not be tolerated. Nonsymbolic violence on the other hand may be an attempt directly to force change in illegal ways, or to threaten the use of force, or it may be, and often is, both at once. Nonsymbolic violence may also be simply an expression of extreme frustration, but then it does not properly fall under a definition which, like the one we have accepted, restricts the notion of political violence to force used with the intention of securing political ends.

As an example of an act of symbolic violence, one might mention the forcible seizure of Alcatraz by American Indians, and its defense by arms, for the purpose of calling attention to the unjust deprivation of Indian lands by the government. Violence of this kind is but a short step from the nonviolent civil disobedience that Rawls believes to be sometimes morally justifiable. It is an attempt, after legal recourse fails, and perhaps nonviolent civil disobedience as well, to appeal directly to principles of justice that are generally acknowledged. If, on the other hand, the Chiricahua Apaches should pillage and burn small white squatter settlements on their reservation, and warn other settlers of the same fate if they do not move out, their action could not readily be accepted as symbolic. It would amount to the use of force and threat of force to accomplish their ends.

Symbolic violence is a way of dramatizing an appeal to justice after the failure of legal recourse, but it is not a way of forcing the change that it is felt justice requires—or not primarily that. If a group places a bomb in a building, it might leave two different kinds of message on the ruins. One might say, "Look at the extremity to which you have driven us! We have been unjustly oppressed, and all avenues of recourse have been closed to us." The other might read, "Unless we are treated more decently, we will henceforth bomb a building each week until our demands are met." The writers of the latter note may no doubt feel that they have been unjustly treated, but they are not by their act appealing to the general sense of justice so much as taking matters into their own hands to right what they feel to be wrongs. Their violent act is not, then, on my definition, a symbolic one.

A consequence of the failure to distinguish symbolic from non-symbolic violence (both of which fit the rough definition of political violence with which we are working) is that justification too easily shades off into sympathetic explanation. There are instances of violence which we can understand, for which we can account in such terms as extreme frustration, fear, and hopeless rage, but which at the same time we cannot justify. Honderich points out that people whose lives are degraded and miserable may resort to violence when they realize that there is no urgency in the headquarters of power which is likely to make a change in their lifetimes. But it does not follow that they are, merely in virtue of this, justified in their decision. Excused, perhaps—if that term is not too patronizing for the circumstances—but not justified.

Nonsymbolic violent action also may sometimes be justified. In times that call for revolution, men have justifiably moved beyond symbolic violence. They have justifiably done so when their cause is just, when all recourse is closed, and when even civil disobedience and symbolic violence have proved fruitless. But I do suggest that a discussion of the justification of political violence which fails to distinguish symbolic from nonsymbolic violence is, by so much, less clear.

Symbolic violence can be justified more readily than nonsymbolic and civil disobedience can be justified more readily than symbolic violence. Civil disobedience has the advantage that its motives are generally not so easy to impugn, and its principled nature consequently not so easily obscured. The advantage obtains on the usual acceptation of violence, according to which there is no loss to the initiator of violence. But it is worth noting that, even if it is a fact that most acts of violence are of this sort, it is but a contingent fact. If a man should immolate himself in the fire he sets at draft headquarters, he might avoid the imputation of unworthy motives (hate, revenge) as successfully as the civil disobedient who pours blood in the files and surrenders to the authorities. The intractable difficulty with symbolic violence is that just because it is violence it creates what Bentham would have called mischief, and sometimes the mischief it must create to draw attention to an injustice will cancel out whatever value it may have had as a symbol. Situations do arise in which privilege is so well entrenched, and the sense of justice so deadened, that the message of symbolic violence will not be read, or if read not taken seriously. Symbolic violence cannot then, remaining symbolic, be elevated by degrees to holocaust. At some point, by whatever appeal of principle it may be accompanied, it transmutes to something unjustifiable and even inexcusable.

Nevertheless, ordinarily the question what is the intent of an act of violence, whether to protest injustice or to force change, is a crucial one where justification is at issue. It seems more likely that men in the original position, aware of the intransigence of power, would leave a place for symbolic violence than that they would permit nonsymbolic violence. In fact, it is difficult to see how a constitution could be written which would allow men who burn with the injustice of their lot to take it into their own hands to alter the balance of burdens and privileges.

NOTES

1.   "On Violence," *Journal of Philosophy* 66 (1969): 602.
2.   *Ibid.*, p. 613.
3.   Certainly no proof is intended (see "Justice as Fairness," *Philosophical Review* 67 [1958]: 174), and it is arguable that all that is at issue is to make clear what kind of principles is in question (*ibid.*, p. 169).
4.   In *Civil Disobedience: Theory and Practice*, ed. Hugo Adam Bedau (New York: Pegasus, 1969), p. 248.

Reply

TED HONDERICH

Rights

There is a kind of man of whom it cannot be said that he acts responsibly or that he is an autonomous moral agent. He is unreflectively obedient. Through further consideration of him, we can see what supposition about a government's right to obedience is in question in Wolff's argument. That right, which is fundamental to the argument, is much talked-of but left unclear. We can find out enough about it by way of the certainty that it is a right which is in fact granted by the unreflectively obedient man.

This man, one can take it, is like the soldier who kills the peasants because he believes that it is right to do whatever his officer commands, without reflecting for himself on other facts about his action. If we take Wolff literally, of course, we have someone else suggested to us, the automatic soldier. He shoots when told, but without even the single conviction of the first soldier. He acts in "submission to the will of another, *irrespective of reasons.*"[1] It is doubtful that there are any such men, but let us pass by any argument attaching to that.

I take it, as does Pincoffs, that it is absurd to say that the only "politically important rights to obedience" that a government may have, perhaps the only "rights to obedience," are morally unacceptable rights to subjects who are like either soldier. More plainly, it is absurd to suppose that we can only attempt to condemn a terrorist who sets a bomb, insofar as we bring in his relationship with government and law, as traditionally conceived in political theory, by the appalling argument that he is *not* behaving like either soldier.

Pincoffs is of the opinion, however, that the other such rights
to obedience noted in my essay are also at least morally questionable, and for the same kind of reason. He supposes, perhaps as a
result of a careless sentence of mine, that these may be described as
rights to reflective as against unreflective obedience. One of them,
thought to be the most defensible or realistic, is a government's
right to have its subjects accept a burden of proof of moral justification if they choose to break the law. However, it is said, this may
go against a principle of responsibility or moral autonomy. A man
may think there is no good reason to accept the burden of proof.

The rights suggested by Pincoffs are not those which I had in
mind. My argument does not depend on the reminder that "what
is commanded [by a government] is reflective rather than unreflective obedience." What I suggest is that if one says that a government has a right to a man's obedience, one may mean the plain
thing that there is an argument for his obeying the government and
that there is a general acceptance of this fact. If one says, in this
way, that a government has a right to a man's obedience, one makes
no mention whatever of a man's reflections or want of them. One
does not assert that he must think for himself or not think for himself. What is set against a right to unreflective obedience is not a
right to reflective obedience but a right to obedient behavior.

There is no doubt that there may be a conflict of a certain kind
between the belief that a government has a right of this kind and,
for example, the belief that the man ought to do what he thinks
right. It is not, of course, a conflict of inconsistency. The conflict
consists partly in the fact that one may not be able to urge the man
to act on both of one's beliefs. None of that, however, falsifies or
impugns the first belief. One can perfectly well go on believing that
there is a reason for obeying the government, even if one admits
that the man must not be false to his beliefs. In contrast, there *is*
inconsistency between the assertion that a government has a right
to unreflective obedience and the assertion that every man must reflect for himself.

What lies behind this dispute, as now seems to me clearer, is that
Wolff and Pincoffs have in mind attitudes and claims of a govern-

ment or its officers. The attitude of a cabinet, a civil servant, or a policeman may well be that people are to do what they are told, whatever they may think about it. Most of us support this attitude in most circumstances. We side with the law against the man who sincerely believes that he has an absolute obligation to shoot people. This attitude may issue in talk of a right to obedience. It is not the talk I have in mind, or the talk that is important to violence and related problems. We can put it all aside and not be deprived of any familiar political arguments against violence—I mean arguments having to do with a man's relationship to government and law, arguments established in political theory.[2]

Law as Command

Pincoffs' second reply has to do with the conception of law as command. Some laws, he rightly notes, do not seem to have the character of commands. I cannot really see that this matter is germane to the dispute or, at any rate, to what I wish to claim. The criminal law certainly can be conceived as a set of commands, as I have. Still, one could take up some different general conception, or none at all, without embarrassment. We suppose a man sets a bomb and thereby breaks a law. We leave aside the question of the general character of law. We have the question of what can be said against him. My view is that it is perfectly sensible to assert that the government has a right to his lawfulness and that an assertion of this kind can derive from political theory. Wolff's view appears to be that if the assertion does so derive, it is the very unsensible assertion that a government has a right to unreflective lawfulness.

Other Conceptions of Violence

Wolff makes observations about conceptions of violence other than the one he describes as the distinctively political one. Classes or groups in society are said to be led by their interests to take up different conceptions. One is the conception of violence as illegality, another is the conception of violence as protest by the Left. Pincoffs describes these conceptions as "literally meaningless," which strikes me as a remarkable falsehood. It is true that there is "no rational ground for choice between them," if that is understood as amounting to a certain evident fact: in part that none of them can be described as necessarily issuing in error. It is false that violence can be correctly defined as puzzlement, but if we do so define it, we do not speak falsely if we assert that violence is a state into which philosophers commonly fall. None of these seems to amount to an argument that could possibly serve, as Pincoffs supposes, to "establish the incoherence of the concept of political violence." That there are different conceptions of violence, and in a sense nothing to choose between them, does not by itself render incoherent *any* concept attached to the term.

Instructive though they are, I cannot see that any of these first three objections to my essay, having to do with rights, law as command, and other conceptions of violence, is successful.

Justice

My discussion of Rawls' doctrines, perhaps through fault of my own, seems misleadingly reported. In the discussion,

1. an ideal society of justice is sketched and a question raised about there being an independent argument for law abidance in it;

2. actual societies, and the duty and the obligation of obedience imposed on their members, are considered. The duty is allowed to derive from the fact that the society makes some approach to equal liberty for all, and some approach to a state of affairs in which favorable inequalities are required in order to have the worst off as well off as they are. It is suggested that it can be argued that movement toward a fuller realization of the two principles sometimes calls for, and justifies, political violence. Further, it is suggested that men would, in a certain situation of ignorance, allow for the possibility of violence in the society they are devising. There is this independent argument for violence if there is an independent argument for law abidance in general;

3. the acceptability of the two principles which are to govern the direction of the societies is questioned. It is suggested, in part, that liberties cannot be regarded as sacrosanct.

My principal arguments against Rawls, then, are that his principles of justice may sanction violence in actual societies, or sanction it more often than he supposes, that men would in a certain situation agree to the possibility of violence in a society to come, whatever such hypotheses about agreements are worth, and that the two principles of justice are not beyond question.

Independent Arguments

Pincoffs objects to the suggestion that if we suppose the hypothetical proposition about agreement does provide an argument for the principles, and a similar proposition provides an argument for law abidance in a society where the principles are partly realized, then we can also suppose that a related proposition provides an argument for some violence—i.e., that rational and self-interested men, engaged in devising institutions and practices for a society to come, would allow for the possibility of political violence. He asks what provisions could possibly be accepted in order to establish this possibility. Certainly our hypothetical assembly would not agree on a general dispensation, an allowance that any man may resort to violence when he feels it to be necessary.

There is no doubt that there is a difficulty. However, it is not insuperable. Certainly it is one of many such difficulties that are to be faced in the general speculation about hypothetical contracts and agreements. To choose the most germane example, Rawls supposes that the hypothetical assembly arrives at guidelines about civil disobedience, as distinct from violence. The assembly agrees that under certain conditions in the society to come, civil disobedience is to be regarded as a possibility. The conditions are in fact sketched.[3] The same can be done, with no intrinsically greater difficulty, for violence. The general enterprise of reaching agreements, incidentally, is not only that of writing a constitution.

Symbolic and Nonsymbolic Violence

This distinction provided by Pincoffs seems to me of value and I have no objection to it. It offers us a further useful characterization of political violence despite the inevitable fact that there are cases which cannot be seen to fall into either of the two categories. I take it that what I described in my essay as nondeterrent violence may include not only symbolic violence but also some nonsymbolic violence. It seems to me important, for particular reasons, to say more about the kind of coercion that enters into typical political violence, but I shall not do so here.[4]

NOTES

1. "On Violence," *The Journal of Philosophy*, 66 (1969): 607. My italics.

2. Wolff allows that even if there can be no "distinctively political right" to a man's abstaining from certain uses of force (those which we ordinarily call acts of violence), there may be *moral* arguments for his abstention. It seems to be taken as obvious that traditional arguments from the nature of democracy, and also the other familiar arguments for lawfulness, are no more than arguments for the distinctively political right: a right to unreflective obedience. It is this that I have been disputing. It would have been as much to the point to dispute the additional implicit suggestion that moral arguments against violence are somehow of secondary importance.

3. *A Theory of Justice* (Oxford: Oxford University Press (Clarendon), 1972), pp. 371–77, 383–84.

4. The matter is discussed in my essay "Democratic Violence," to appear in the proceedings of the Third International Conference on the History of Ideas, 1972.

Disruption of the Judicial Process

GRAHAM HUGHES

I

Both the conservative and the liberal strains in the Anglo-American tradition have at times agreed in holding the judge and the court in some considerable reverence. For the conservative, the court may appear as the solid guardian of law and order in a disorderly world. For the liberal, at least in the United States, courts have often seemed to be the only branch of government that could be viewed with any enthusiasm. In the last twenty years, when the legislature and the executive dragged their feet, was it not the courts who moved to end discrimination, who gave a panoply of rights to suspects and defendants, who ended rotten boroughs and ordered reapportionment? Take away the liberal faith in the courts and the last bastion is down.

Both conservatives and liberals thus share a sense of dismay at recent outbreaks of disruptive behavior by defendants in the courtroom. How should we react to defendants who will not cooperate with the judicial process, to blacks who shout insults at judges, to white radicals who mount guerrilla theater in the courtroom? Can we rest content with the gag and the nightstick as the inevitable countermoves, or even with more sophisticated suggestions of plastic cages or closed circuit television relay of the proceedings to a defendant outside the courtroom, free to communicate with his counsel by telephone? Most discussion so far has been in terms of a choice between such alternatives, and there can, of course, be no escape from debate about the rival merits of restraint and separation once disruption is on the scene. But to accept disruption in the court as just another of the seven plagues which annually visit our sick society, to concentrate in a monocular fashion on anodynes and palliatives, while neglecting thoughtful discussion of the roots of the disorder, would be a serious error.

In the first place it is of primary importance to know whether the disruptors feel themselves to be acting in a *justifiable* manner or whether they are simply savages who live outside our realm of discourse. Their own justifications and any others which might be supplied for them will deserve the most serious examination, for any conclusion that some form of disruption in our courtrooms might in some circumstances be justified would be a startling one, inevitably entailing urgent duties to reform institutions and practices so as to remove the causes.

But before considering the question of disruption itself, we must first say a few introductory words about the general obligation of the citizen to obey the law and the possible exemptions allowed by a theory of civil disobedience. For, while the phenomenon of disruption in the courts appears to owe most to a theory of revolution, I want to contend that it may also, at least sometimes, be regarded as a legitimate extension of an acceptable theory of civil disobedience.

For these purposes I shall find it useful to adopt an approach to civil disobedience which I derive from the writing of John Rawls and Richard Wasserstrom and which is connected with a modernized version of social-contract theory. This approach concedes that any person who participates in society and derives benefits and protections from the scheme of mutual forebearances erected by the legal system has at least a *prima facie* moral obligation in return to go along with the decisions which are validly made under the rules of the system. But it insists at the same time that the obligation cannot be more than a *prima facie* one. There is no reason in logic or moral principle why even a system which functions with perfect, formal democratic validity should be able to make *any* demand on a citizen or to call for *any* sacrifice from him simply because he has derived benefits from the system. This is not after all a business of selling one's soul to the devil. What the system may properly demand is that the citizen recognize the initial *prima facie* duty to comply and the consequent burden of proof on him to justify disobedience by some compelling ethical argument. So it would clearly be inadequate for discharging this burden for the citizen to show only that compliance with the law would be inconvenient for him or that he himself takes a different view of the prudence of the law from that obviously taken by the legislature when they passed it. Part of the burden imposed by the social compact is the obligation to comply even when this may be personally inconvenient or contrary to one's own prudential judgment. But if the citizen after reflection should take the view that compliance with the law would result in his submitting to fundamental injustice or, perhaps worse, in his having to do fundamental injustice to another, it is not at all so clear that he does not now have a reason for refusing which can be accommodated within the political theory of the social contract.

What this amounts to is a contention that someone disobeying the law while asserting such a justification is acting morally. It does not, of course, contend that there is a legal right to disobey nor even that the taking of legal steps against the disobedient is morally unjustifiable. The morality of an individual's adherence to the dictates of his conscience must be weighed socially against other communal interests which might be undermined by taking no notice of his action. But, at the least, the recognition that the individual is acting morally is an important consideration to be assessed by law enforcement officials in exercising the discretionary function of deciding whether or not to prosecute and by a judge in determining what sanction to apply.

This initial brief glance at civil disobedience may seem at first to be little connected with the principal theme of disruption of the judicial process, for those who have been most active in sabotaging the tranquility of the courtroom do not, at first sight, look like civil disobedients in the senses in which we have so far been using the term. In the history of ideas there are, however, two vital connections here. The first is that the question of submission to the judi-

cial process has for some time been coming to a head in the literature and practice of civil disobedience. And, second, the disruptive
activities that have taken place in the courtroom, while not consequent upon earlier acts of classical disobedience, may in themselves
be viewed as a kind of protest which, if it can be justified at all,
will have to be justified by arguments which owe a great deal to
the traditional discussions of civil disobedience. For those who
have embarked upon disruptive behavior have certainly viewed
themselves as demonstrating against injustices which could not be
denounced in any other way.

II

In the classical, Gandhian concept of civil disobedience, the willingness to submit to the civil power and accept punishment for the
breach of the law is part of the appeal to conscience by which
the disobedient draws attention to the wrong and offers himself as
the sacrifice which ought to shock good and conscientious citizens
and officials into an awareness of the need for change. But on the
American scene, the notions of sacrifice and accepting punishment
have become clouded over by social and political complexities.

We might begin here by asking a preliminary question which
may help us to work our way gradually towards the question of disruption. Ought a civil disobedient simply to plead guilty and not
defend at all against a prosecution? I would submit that such a
requirement is surely not a necessary component of fidelity to the
ideals of civil disobedience for, although he may be ready to admit doing the act, the disobedient's whole purpose is to assert reasons for doing it, and the forum for proclaiming these reasons and
making his appeal to conscience would be closed down by a guilty
plea. If then he may plead not guilty, is he under a moral duty to
abstain from raising any legal defenses? Must he raise only moral
justifications for doing the act and not seek in any other way to
escape a judgment of technical guilt? Again the affirmative is not
obviously the only right answer, for the disobedient's moral positions may often overlap with contentions of constitutional privilege,

so that his assertion that he is legally not guilty may be an exact statement of his moral position.

If we can go thus far and accept the propriety of the disobedient's raising defenses of a constitutional dimension, can we include within this the raising of ancillary constitutional-procedural matters which do not go to the core of his moral position? For example, may he properly contend that the evidence offered by the prosecution was illegally seized or that there was some impropriety in the grand jury proceedings? This is more difficult, since such arguments would seem to dim the appeal to conscience and sidetrack the proceeding down another path. And yet the disobedient might argue that his general stance is that of a champion of justice and fairness in society and that this includes his own right to have a legal and fair trial. For, if he is willing to be convicted, this is only provided that the conviction be according to law. Part of what he insists upon in his appeal to conscience is that the state should behave in a lawful and constitutional manner. There is, of course, the risk (if that is the right word) that the successful raising of an objection to the prosecution's procedures may be sufficiently decisive to result in an acquittal. Here indeed there may be a choice to be made, since the defendant may take the view that the value to be preserved by holding the prosecution to full legal propriety in its presentation of the case against him is outweighed by the added strength that his appeal to conscience will gain from conviction and submission to punishment. But the contrary choice, though it may have the practical outcome of diluting the strength of the appeal to conscience, is not irreconcilable with the initial posture of civil disobedience.

In the context of disruption the preceding discussion leads us on to ask whether the ideals of civil disobedience involve a general duty of submission to judicial process. Certainly the orthodox view is that they do. Eugene Rostow has written recently:

> If a man decides to commit an act of civil disobedience, for example, because he feels that what the law requires would breach his obligation to God, our culture would acknowledge at most his naked pow-

er, but not his right or privilege to do so. But then he should in turn acknowledge that if he decides to violate the law he thereby breaches a covenant with moral dimensions and is not committing a purely technical offense. To be sure, he would contend that he is breaking the law in order to avoid what he would regard as a greater sin. But the law, too, has a moral content; it represents the moral judgment of the majority, and its sense of justice. Under such circumstances, the individual should at least respect his duty to the law he has helped to make by accepting its penalties.[1]

But it is perfectly possible to contemplate a society in which a duty to submit to judicial process is not so apparent. Should those who illegally (in the positive law sense) opposed the Nazi regime in Germany have offered themselves sacrificially to Nazi judicial processes? Manifestly not. Here it might be said that the Nazi example is of a regime so fundamentally shot through with evil, partiality, and a lack of any expectation of fair treatment that the situation was one going far beyond the ethics of civil disobedience, one where revolution was justified and where all duties of cooperation ceased. Such a statement begins to sharpen the outlines of what is surely a most central question for our discussion—is refusal to cooperate with the judicial process only morally justifiable in a situation where the regime as a whole is so unredeemable that revolution is justified?

Anxiety and uneasiness about the proper answer to this question have been apparent of late in liberal and radical discussions of illegal action arising out of protests against the war in Vietnam. At the trial of Dr. Spock and others in 1968, the defendants were criticized by some radical commentators for beclouding their moral stance by conducting a fairly conventional defense which relied largely on arguments of a constitutional and procedural nature. A more uncertain, wait-and-see position was put forward by Noam Chomsky and others, writing in the *New York Review of Books*: "It is not true that . . . the courts are merely serving as an instrument of tyranny and repression. At the same time these institutions are not functioning in an acceptable fashion. . . . The objective circumstances do not warrant a refusal to take part in the judicial or political process. . . . The situation is ambiguous and the problems of acting responsibly are frustrating."[2]

The notes of doubt and hesitation in this passage leave its implications unclear, but it is not difficult to move from it to the position that only two alternatives are available to the protestor of injustice—either he follows the traditional path of civil disobedience which requires at the least cooperation with the judicial process if not full admission of guilt, or he takes to the barricades and commits himself to revolution. Certainly those defendants who have recently disrupted court proceedings have not been civil disobedients in the orthodox sense and might be happy to style themselves revolutionaries. But I believe these alternatives are too stark and unaccommodating and that there is a third position which, although fragile and difficult of precise statement, needs to be put forward.

III

To begin with, it is possible to imagine a situation in which refusal to cooperate with the judicial process would be the only kind of civil disobedience that would make much sense. Suppose a society where all the laws are generally acknowledged to be wise and just, where the legislators are prudent and incorruptible, the police and prosecutors gentle and humane, and where no great economic inequalities exist. This utopia is, however, marred (and perhaps made more believable) by the circumstance that some of its courts are staffed by corrupt and arbitrary judges whose improper and unpredictable conduct of judicial proceedings is left uncorrected by a weak and also corrupt appellate court system. Any defendant brought before these courts can have no reasonable expectation that his case will be decided by a rational application of the rules and principles of law to the facts. If efforts to unseat such judges through constitutional means should fail, then it seems that refusal to cooperate peacefully with their processes becomes at the least a moral right and perhaps a moral duty for the good citizen. This is only to say simply that where the judicial process as a whole or some part of it loses integrity, then it forfeits its claim to respect and submission.

And yet such a situation might well not be one where a general revolutionary policy would be justified. The excrescence would be such that it could most appropriately and perhaps only effectively be protested by disobedience in the context of the judicial process, and yet the excrescence might not be so general and so pervasive in all aspects of the regime that revolution would be justified. A dictatorial and brutal regime could conceivably (though not probably) coexist with reasonably fair and impartial courts. South Africa may be such an example. Here revolution may be justified even though the judicial process is comparatively unexceptionable. Conversely, a reasonably socially fair and just society might in some aspects be saddled with grave abuses in its judiciary and courts. Here, although revolution might not be justified, noncooperation with courts might be.

So the argument begins to develop that disruption in the courts *could* be (in certain given circumstances) a justifiable form of civil disobedience which does not depend on the prior identification and justification of a generally revolutionary position. Would such a posture be justifiable only when the iniquity protested against was in the judge himself and his conduct of the courtroom? Could it extend to situations of more diffuse failure of integrity in the legal system? We might begin here by offering a concrete illustration in a comparatively trivial area without obvious connotations of radicalism and certainly far removed from traditional contexts of civil disobedience.

Suppose that a state has a very broadly drawn statute which prohibits all forms of gambling. Local law enforcement authorities have long been in the habit of ignoring public gambling activities conducted by religious groups for charitable or church related fund raising and also ignoring fairly overt social poker playing for money. However, a fairly rigorous policy of enforcement is pursued with respect to dice games played for money. Now it so happens that, while middle-class WASPS, Irish, and Italians commonly play cards, dice games are usually played by blacks and Spanish-speaking Americans. These minority groups thus bear the brunt of prosecutions and naturally feel aggrieved. They try to redress this grievance in an orderly and democratic fashion by addressing arguments to the police and local prosecutors, urging a change in the selective enforcement policies. These are of no avail. When prosecuted for gambling offenses, they appeal the convictions and make constitutional arguments that the selective law enforcement policies are an infringement of their rights to equal protection of the laws and due process. These arguments fail, and the convictions are affirmed.

At this point there are plausible grounds for contending that, with respect to gambling laws, an unjust and unequal enforcement policy has been countenanced by the law and the courts so that on this issue at least the usual moral arguments in favor of cooperating with judicial processes have been overborne by countervailing arguments derived from principles of justice and fairness. Here again we begin to find a case for starting civil disobedience in the courtroom, but again this is not at all the same as a general case for revolution or a general argument for behaving criminally or even a general argument for always violating the tranquility of the courts. It asserts only that in one small and very particular context the administration of justice has generally deteriorated into arbitrary caprice and deserves no respect. It would be a perfectly proper position to be maintained by a generally law-abiding and orderly group.

The courtroom disruption which has emerged recently and which is now so concerning authorities and legal writers has not, of course, been in the low-level context of gambling offenses. But the arguments made above may have even more force in the context in which disruptions have actually occurred.

IV

Radical polemicists routinely contend that the United States is a society shot through with racism and social injustice. Those who have disrupted courtroom procedures would no doubt agree with this condemnation. But, if their censure of American society were expressed only in such general terms, without any particular focus on the operation of the legal system, then their position *vis-à-vis* disruption would amount to either or both of the following arguments: (1) Where pervasive social injustice and racism exist so as to justify a revolutionary position, then, as part of the general strategy and tactics of revolution, it is proper to refuse to cooperate with the courts even though the judiciary and other organs of the legal system generally conduct themselves in a fair and equitable manner. (2) Where people are brought before courts as a result of the operation of laws which impinge on them in an unjust and racist manner because of their socioeconomic background and race, then, even though a general revolutionary posture may not be justified and even though the courts themselves behave in a fair and equitable manner, nevertheless noncooperation with the judicial process is justified as a form of civil disobedience designed to evangelize the community as to the injustice protested against.

The first position is one that lawyers, as lawyers, can have nothing to say about, though of course as individuals lawyers too may make the choice to espouse revolution, as did Dr. Castro. The second position would be a fairly uncomplicated extension of general civil disobedience theory as it has been outlined earlier. Again it would be a situation where no specific charges were levelled against the processes of the courts as such and where, consequently, lawyers in their professional capacity would not be in a position to remedy the evil protested against. If any merit is found in the arguments of the noncooperators or disruptors here though, lawyers might be said to have a special moral duty to draw this to the attention of the public and other branches of government and to lobby for legislative and other reforms which would eliminate or dilute the legitimacy of the complaint. If, for example, lawyers become convinced that the whole edifice of narcotics laws can for the most part be seen as a stupidly brutal, unjustly discriminatory, and hopelessly inefficient penal substitute for needed social reforms, then lawyers have a peculiar and inescapable duty to press this point of view upon the community and the legislatures. If some defendants in some category of cases of this kind should disrupt court proceedings, then lawyers must no doubt proceed in an orderly fashion to take what steps may be necessary to continue with the hearing, but at the same time they must perceive in their own professional context the justifying circumstances which make punitive sanctions against disruption inappropriate and which should persuade lawyers to act as apologists for those who disrupt.

V

In fact, the moral concern of lawyers with the circumstances which impel people to disruption of court proceedings need not be as remote as that outlined above. For the arguments of the disruptors would surely not exempt the courts and other organs of the legal system from indictment as was done in the hypothetical arguments advanced above. In practice, all institutions, offices, and organs of the criminal law enforcement and adjudicatory systems are very much a part of, if not central in, the American system against which the radical protestors mount their attack. Let us enumerate a series of charges made so frequently and pervasively that they scarcely need documentation—some of them are made peculiarly by blacks, some by political radicals, some by all outside the middle class.

It is alleged that police have murdered black militants and that investigatory and prosecutorial authorities have not made serious attempts to bring these police criminals to justice.

Extensive use is made of police undercover agents in infiltrating radical groups, and the claim is made that these police agents in fact often act as *agents provocateurs*. Police are said to bring framed charges based on concocted evidence against black militants and other radicals. Even where there is a technical basis for properly bringing a charge against such defendants, the prosecutions may often represent gross instances of selective law enforcement. Black prisoners, radical prisoners, and poor prisoners are, it is alleged, sometimes beaten while in detention, and judges and prosecutors and police officials seem unwilling or unable to redress this wrong. Defendants with a radical political connection often meet judges who set impossibly high bail which in practice condemns them to a long incarceration before a verdict is reached or even before their trial begins. It is contended that juries are still unrepresentative, through a combination of the nature of jury lists and the use of peremptory challenges by the prosecutors. Grand juries, it is claimed, are particularly unrepresentative and out of balance. Impartial observers sometimes conclude that judicial conduct of trials of politically radical defendants sometimes falls short of the proper standard of impartiality. Defense attorneys may be harassed; the contempt power is wielded too generously; sentences may seem harsh and punitive in the worst sense.

If all or some of these allegations are sometimes true, it is equally clear that they are not all true all of the time. But even a fair measure of validity here would add up to a serious breakdown of law and order in that most crucial of all areas—the behavior of law enforcement officers and judges. It is also very significant that most of the abuses alleged here are not very susceptible to correction by an appellate court. An identifiable body of people who find themselves subjected with some consistency to the practices outlined above can bring not unpersuasive moral arguments for their legitimate exemption from usual duties of cooperation with the processes of the legal system.

It is the above kind of argument which I believe underlies a good deal of radical rhetoric and especially Black Panther rhetoric. Recently a number of distinguished and generally liberal writers have expressed astonishment that anyone could seriously put forward a demand that the murder trial of Black Panthers in New Haven should be brought to an end and the defendants freed. After all, they have pointed out, there appears to be a respectable *prima facie* case which, without prejudging the guilt of the defendants, at least warrants a trial. Taking slogans shouted at meetings and wall graffiti at their face value, this apparently calm and deliberative response seems unanswerable. But the quiet, reflective tone which is certainly eminently to be desired for intellectual debate is not quite appropriate for the mass political meeting and generally not well suited for the radical who wishes to activate a poor, socially depressed, and semi-literate constituency. "Off the Pigs" and "Free Bobby" are indeed mindless shouts, but inarticulately buried beneath them we may detect the shape of a reasonably viable moral argument of the kind I have tried to sketch here.

If the argument presented stands up at all, then it will not be a sufficient response to say that the system generally is sound, even if gravely flawed, because the contention here is that one segment of the system may be so gravely flawed that those on whom it impinges in a certain well enough defined context are so reasonably devoid of any expectation of fair and equal treatment that they no longer have any reason to cooperate. If people are to trust the system, then in the long run it must show itself to be worthy of trust.

VI

The main theme of this discussion has been that disruption in the courts is either the expression of a generally revolutionary position or, in a less extreme posture, a kind of civil disobedience evincing protest against what are felt to be deep injustices either in the processes which have brought defendants before the courts or in the court procedures themselves. The disruption which has so far attracted the most attention has stemmed from defendants who probably espouse a generally revolutionary position, though this would no doubt encompass the belief that there are basic injustices in the law enforcement system and judicial procedures. Lawyers in their professional capacities cannot be expected to find general social remedies for revolutionary protests, except insofar as revolutionary positions owe something to basic injustices in the content and operation of the legal system itself. But where disruption is not so much a byproduct of a general commitment to revolution but is rather an *ad hoc* response to scarifying malfunctions and inequities in the legal system, then lawyers have a peculiarly urgent duty to make the correct response.

For here there are two incipient dangers both of which have already to some extent come to the surface. The first is that persistent indifference by the legal community to the legitimate griev-, ances of defendants, particularly in large urban areas, will so deepen and sharpen the sense of injustice that disruption of legal procedures will become the norm and not the exception. The recent disturbances in Houses of Detention in New York City lend credence to this conjecture. Courtroom disruption may soon become the tactic not only of a handful of committed revolutionaries but of hosts of the black and Spanish-American urban poor who find themselves thrown into the jaws of the so slowly masticating legal monster. Crisis reaction on the part of the legal community will then be seen by the consumers of the legal product for what it is— a coerced response to the violence of men whom the law has made desperate and not the timely correction of perceived injustice. The second, and in the long run the more dangerous, consequence is that those who find the legal system so cynically wanting in qualities of humanity and concern, even wanting in simple efficiency, will soon be converted to a position of supporting general revolution. In this way, as has so often happened in history, a cold and cruel process of law will breed its own destroyers.

The claustrophobic effect induced by the mental furniture which a classical legal education and the practice of law often provide may lead to a response to disruption in the courtroom which may be tragically irrelevant to the present scene. When confronted by an incident of disruption or when contemplating its possibility, lawyers are apt to think in terms of the rending of the very, basic fabric of law and order. The courtroom is likened to a temple, and disruptors are seen as almost committing sacrilege. The judicial process for the lawyer is the ultimate happening, in which all the argument and all the disputation is resolved by authoritative rulings. If this very *sanctum sanctorum* can be invaded, if rude hands, as it were, seek to dash the chalice from the priest, then all the rest is of no avail. An emotional response of shock is thus very understandable but is, for that reason, all the more in need of a cool analysis in the light of a reality which is not exclusively apprehended through the eyes of a keeper of the temple.

The first step is to perceive and acknowledge with due humility that some part of the response of outrage is due to the simple professional vanity of people who are accustomed to thinking of their life's work as carrying a peculiar dignity, status, and social value, and who are therefore correspondingly filled with rage at those who demonstrate in the most brusque and pointed manner that they do not agree. Some of this is encapsulated in the traditional phrase "contempt of court," which suggests unhappily that the heart of the offense of disruption is an insult to the profession. In the only recent English case which has had to deal with disruption in the courtroom, Mr. Justice Salmon made just this point,

> The archaic description of these proceedings as "contempt of court" is in my view unfortunate and misleading. It suggests that they are designed to buttress the dignity of the judges and to protect them from insult. Nothing could be further from the truth. No such protection is needed. The sole purpose of proceedings for contempt is to give our courts the power effectively to protect the rights of the public by ensuring that the administration of justice shall not be obstructed or prevented.[3]

As the English judge so rightly points out there are, of course, patently legitimate public interests which demand that steps be taken to avoid disruption in the courtroom and perhaps, in some cases, to punish it. But if it is a public interest that is being protected, then the true nature and limits of that interest must be located. It is submitted that these are to be found in the interest of the public in having a tranquil legal process, *so long as that process is by and large just and humane.* When the process loses to a considerable extent the qualities of justice and humanity, at that moment the general public interest in its tranquility disappears.

NOTES

1. Rostow, "No Right to Civil Disobedience," *Trial* 6 (1970): 16.
2. Noam Chomsky, Paul Lauter, and Florence Howe, "Reflections on a Political Trial," *New York Review of Books* 11 (1968): 23.
3. "Morris v. Master of the Crown Office," *Weekly Law Reports* 2 (1970): 792, 801.

Comments: Some Moral Perspective on Defying Legal Authority

HYMAN GROSS

Recognizing a right to defy public authority is an important and highly sophisticated moral achievement in any community. Occasions on which the right has been exercised while still unrecognized are among the most sublime moments in human history. But defying authority, which is a commonplace and multifarious practice everywhere and at all times, though it may be commended for amusement and for psychological gratification, is when without good cause never morally commendable. And there are times when it deserves condemnation both legally and morally as a social harm because it frustrates procedures for resolving problems in the public domain in ways which accord with the common good.

It is a matter of the first importance, then, to give definition to the right of defiance. Hughes has raised disturbing questions that bear on this right when it is asserted in derogation of the authority of the very institution in the legal system principally responsible for legal recognition of the right. My discussion is in three parts. I think, as Hughes evidently does, that it is important in the first place to assess the extent of the moral commitment to legal authority that may rightly be required from members of the community, but I disagree that there is a *prima facie* moral obligation to obey the law. My reasons for this and my notion of what moral commitment there is to legal authority are given in the first section. Professor Hughes has offered a number of points in justification of courtroom disruption, and these are given critical examination in the second part. Finally, I wish to suggest what seem to me to be proper moral grounds for claiming that a disruption ought not to result in liability to punishment, or at least that punishment ought to be mitigated.

I

As I understand it, Hughes' view of civil disobedience starts with a recognition of a *prima facie* moral obligation to obey the law. This obligation derives from a kind of social contract and represents the exacting of a *quid pro quo*: one who takes benefit from a system of rules governing others with whom one lives must himself benefit others by submitting to the governance of those rules. But this moral obligation is only *prima facie*, and when conscience signals that the rules work a serious injustice the moral obligation of obedience is suspended.

There are two things here that cause me difficulty. One is the notion of *obedience* to law. The other is the assertion of a *prima facie* moral obligation respecting law.

First, the matter of obedience. It does indeed make perfect sense to speak of the law-abiding citizen as obeying the law, conforming his conduct to the rules, complying with orders, and in general doing those things that satisfy the lawful demands of public authority. The picture of the citizen's role in the legal order as essentially one of submission to authority is congenial to many who wish to uphold the claims of authority as well as to many who wish to spurn them. But it is seriously misleading, not in what it portrays, but in what it neglects. By giving exclusive attention to the idea of obedience it fails to notice that with regard to both its processes and content the law has been derived and must continue to be derived from something shared by members of the community which I shall call social intelligence.

There are, in the first place, standards of official practice for the legal system which determine how legal authority in its various forms should be exercised. These standards, though different in kind, are no less part of the legal system than the very rules that confer authority. As a system of authority the law is only one among many on the social scene, though it is the most comprehensive by virtue of its being the only one whose powers are entirely self-limited. Its standards of official practice derive from the same social intelligence that defines the operation of other systems of authority in society.

In the second place, the content of the law is determined by social intelligence. Though getting information about authoritative determinations may require consulting someone trained as a legal specialist, comprehending the grounds is within the competence of the ordinary citizen. Indeed all members of the community have the capacity to make and criticize legal determinations which those in authority make authoritatively. The reason is that the law is simply a public employment of the social intelligence which is constantly used privately by each citizen in his dealings with others. If this were not the case it would be a monstrous injustice to make answerable to the law for its conduct a citizenry not learned in the law. But in fact we do not consider it unjust that, for example, most persons prosecuted under a penal provision were not familiar with it at the time they are alleged to have committed the crime.

Now *obedience* is a strikingly inapposite way of characterizing the role of the citizen in this regard. One cannot *obey* determinations reached by the exercise of social intelligence any more than one can obey rules of grammar, standards of medical practice, or principles of navigation. When there is an authoritative statement requiring conformity in these matters, we speak quite properly about obedience or disobedience, but then only with respect to the act requiring conformity and by extension the authority whose act it is. The question remains, regarding the law, whether what is called for morally in the first instance is obedience. I am quite clear that it is not. As Hughes has observed, it is not a matter of selling one's soul to the devil; and unless those in legal authority were supernally wise and just, a primal obligation to submit to their authority would be just that. Whatever moral obligation of this sort there might be must surely derive from that other and morally worthy aspect of law.

I want to say something now about the notion of *prima facie* moral obligation. I know of no stronger argument than the one adopted by Hughes. According to it an item of law has a moral claim on us once its status as law is certified, because it is part of an arrangement of mutual forbearance in the interest of the protection of all. We may conceive this as a social compact to which, as beneficiaries, we are parties. I can readily accept this in a conditional form. *If* laws (and I mean official requirements of all sorts in the legal system) were parts of a general arrangement of this sort, then there would be grounds for such *prima facie* moral obligation. But in my view this condition is not met. In view of the *normal* political processes in our society, the conditional statement of obligation is one which is contrary to fact. Laws are normally created and enforced to satisfy demands of expediency so limited that conceiving them as part of general social arrangements for the common good is indulging in mythical thinking. Putting this in terms to suit the metaphor, we might say that what goes on in the operation of our legal institutions could hardly have been within the contemplation of the parties to the social contract when agreement to abide by the pronouncements of those institutions was given. If it were, there would have to be, I think, a presumption of madness at the time of contract, which would be an alternative ground for defeating the claim of obligation.

The notion of a moral obligation to obey the law because it is the law is widespread and persistent. In doubting the existence of such an obligation I do not for a moment deny that the community at large entertains beliefs which amount to affirming the existence of such an obligation. Polls would show, I have no doubt, that overwhelming numbers think that laws should be obeyed and are strongly disposed to condemn as wrongdoers those who break laws simply because they have broken the law, quite apart from condemnation for the wrongdoing prohibited by law. A minority would accept the *prima facie* qualification which Hughes advocates, so that when fundamental injustice would result from obedience, the obligation to obey would be suspended. But with or without the qualification, the obligation is an item of positive morality which, I contend, will not withstand the test of moral criticism. I think it altogether unreasonable that moral obligation should automatically attach to all the legal products of a process as morally blighted by venality, opportunism, unprincipled compromise, demagoguery, and sheer incompetence as our political process often is. I do not say that the product is normally blighted, only that what produces it cannot claim a moral stature sufficient to create moral obligation by its very hallmark.

Is there moral obligation regarding law? Obviously there is. Things morally obligatory remain so when required by law, though nothing becomes a moral obligation simply by virtue of being legally required. But matters are not quite that simple. There are moral obligations, regrettably very much understated, that surround official acts, that is, acts which are an exercise of legal authority. When such obligations are transgressed, official acts are morally objectionable. There are two general grounds of such moral objectionability. One is the nature of what is being required or allowed in an exercise of legal authority. The other relates to the very act by legal authority of requiring or allowing a certain sort of thing. When the moral objection to an official act receives legal backing, as it does in constitutional and other law, there is then a legal objection to the act and that extinguishes any legal obligation under it, though indeed any moral obligation which there still might be would remain unimpaired in cases where moral objectionability exists only because of the official intervention. When an exercise of legal authority is morally objectionable, there is a moral obligation to refrain from such official acts, and to some extent such moral obligations have been made legal requirements by laws punishing official misconduct and by laws prescribing unobjectionable ways in which legal authority must be exercised.

I have denied that there is any general moral obligation respecting acts that bear legal authority, but have indicated that the law is heavily involved with moral obligations. There is still something further to be said about moral commitment to law in general. Putting it as an extreme generality, I would say acts that make the law what it ought to be are on that account morally right, and acts that make it what it ought not to be are on that account morally wrong.

This standard applies equally to those who exercise legal authority and to those over whom it is exercised.

Now the civil disobedient is one who acts in deliberate defiance of legal authority under the claim of a moral right to do so. (I do not consider as civil disobedients those who violate the law under a claim of a moral right but not in deliberate defiance of authority, as in cases of refusing to have one's child attend school, refusing to submit to inoculation, and the usual selective conscientious objection cases. In these cases a person said to violate the law intends only to enjoy his right, not vindicate an objection to the exercise of legal authority.) The civil disobedient claims a moral right to act in defiance of authority because the exercise of authority being defied is purported to violate a moral obligation. As we noted already, the legal system sometimes accepts such claims and confers on them the status of law. Therefore in the first instance the morally sound move is to seek vindication of one's position through legal procedures. If there is not such vindication, one of two things is then indicated. If the failure to vindicate is itself a morally objectionable exercise of legal authority, acts in defiance of that authority are morally sound; but if such failure to vindicate is not morally objectionable, there is no moral right of defiance.

I wish now to employ the perspective gained from the foregoing discussion to examine what Hughes suggests may tend to justify courtroom disruption as a form of civil disobedience.

II

Hughes poses first the case of a society whose government is utterly benign except for a thoroughly malignant judicial system (though he does not tell us how the wise and just laws of the prudent and incorruptible legislators allow for such a judiciary). The extreme remedy of revolution would entail the regrettable waste of good government—as well, I suppose, as ingratitude—and so civil disobedience directed toward the judicial process makes more sense. I heartily agree that such civil disobedience is justified. When the apparatus of justice simply does not exist, not only is there no moral constraint of participation upon the good citizen, but there is moral cause to defy the empty pretense in the interest of developing a true apparatus of justice. Legal requirements that such authority not be defied would be official immorality, since they would be attempts to coerce obedience to despotism.

Hughes speaks next about a system-wide collapse of justice but with reference to only a single law enforcement policy. He gives as an example selective law enforcement in which gambling laws are enforced mainly against members of certain minority groups though many others in the community gamble. Attempts to nullify convictions as constitutionally objectionable are pursued through appellate procedures, but they fail.

It must be observed that all just and prudent law enforcement is selective. Discretionary powers must be used in all phases of law enforcement so that enforcement accords with an intelligent appreciation of the social evils whose curtailment is the purpose of the law, especially in view of the limited police, prosecutorial, court, detention, and correctional resources available. No less important, these discretionary powers must be exercised in the interest of individual justice with due regard for *prima facie* indications of culpability. Sticking to Hughes' example, I can imagine a sound discretionary policy of enforcement of gambling laws that is aimed at prevention of the violent crime that commonly accompanies certain forms of gambling activity, and also is aimed at destroying revenue to organized crime. The brunt of prosecution might well fall heavily on members of certain ethnic groups and not on others who have also violated the law, and yet equal protection and due process guarantees do not seem to be violated. Income tax evasion is widespread at all social and economic levels above the lowest, and law enforcement efforts are rightly directed to maximize curtailment of the social evil even though this places the brunt of prosecution at the upper socioeconomic level. Prosecutions for violations of law that would normally not be prosecuted are undertaken against reputed leaders of organized crime to take them out of circulation. The brunt of prosecution falls heavily on Italian-

Americans, according to recent protests by organizations of that minority group. The fact is inescapable, furthermore, that crime is of epidemic proportions among the urban poor and is a far more serious problem in these communities than in others. While it may well be that a greater allocation of governmental resources ought to be made to eliminate the causes of such crime, such resources as are allocated for law enforcement are properly used when they are in large measure directed to crimes committed in these communities and elsewhere by some of its members, though this does indeed result in a relatively large proportion of arrests of members of the ethnic and socioeconomic groups most numerous in these communities. The general point here is that if the legal system is concerned to act reasonably—that is if appellate procedures raising constitutional issues of discriminatory law enforcement, for example, are not perfunctory shams—defiance of its authority is not justified simply because there is not equal distribution of prosecution according to race, religion, national origin, social status, and perhaps even sex. If it is the case that the system is no longer concerned with doing justice, and even if this applies only to isolated law enforcement policies, I agree with Hughes that civil disobedience is justified and for the same reasons as in the previous circumstances. If he believes that in fact there is a collapse *of* the legal system regarding some context of law enforcement in America today, I would be very interested to learn of it. I know of none, though I do know of many grave failings and abuses *in* the legal system that must be corrected.

Regarding revolution, I would agree with Hughes that lawyers as lawyers cannot decide whether courtroom disruption to further the ends of revolution is justified, since whether revolution is justified is not a legal question. But I think the importance of the enterprise of justificatory argument in assessing demands for and against revolutionary change cannot be neglected by any sane society. Lawyers as lawyers develop and use such arguments in ways crucial to controversy, and depriving issues of revolution of such rational procedures would be a great misfortune. Just such an intervention on the revolutionary scene by lawyers two hundred years ago in this country had quite beneficial results.

Hughes next suggests, I think, that there is some justification for courtroom disruption deriving from misguided policies which have inhumane effects, illustrated by narcotics laws. His suggestion seems to be very tentative, and if this is so, I would guess it is because he recognizes that the claim of bad policy cannot in itself justify defiance of legal authority. I am not at all clear, furthermore, that a defendant is entitled to have the poor policy being served by the law considered even in mitigation of punishment when the punishment is for contempt of court, as Hughes suggests. The wisdom and justice of a policy of the law *is* a proper consideration in mitigating punishment for the offense constituted by breaking that law. But that is something quite different.

Finally, Hughes considers charges of systematic official misconduct and institutional malfunction which if the case, he says, would support a moral argument for an exemption from the usual duties of cooperation with the processes of the legal system for an identifiable body of people who find themselves victimized with some consistency.

Hughes does not furnish an example of such mass legal antagonism, but refers to the fact of its frequent allegation in black and white radical polemics. If the legal order were in effect such a conspiracy of malice and indifference, for reasons already presented, I think defiance of it is not only justifiable, but commendable. I am, however, less persuaded than Hughes seems to be of the probable truth of a significant portion of these allegations. I think there are explanations of their persistence and passionate declaration other than their truth—explanations shifting attention to the state of mind of those making the declaration—and I am persuaded that these explanations are at least worth investigating when I observe that radical polemics allege similar mass and systematic antagonism in almost every organized part of society. If it should turn out that the belief in a system which tends essentially to injustice is incorrect, the serious failings and abuses which we do have will be seen more clearly for what they really are, and this will greatly facilitate the urgent business of correcting them.

III

The conclusion to be drawn from what has been said so far is that courtroom disruption is a form of morally justifiable civil disobedience when, but only when, full procedures have been undertaken to vindicate legally the position of the one on whose account the disruption is made and such attempted vindication has failed by virtue of morally objectionable official conduct, or by virtue of a lack of meaningful opportunity in the legal system for vindication. On such occasions the law, if it is to be morally sound, must recognize the right of the disrupter and give it effect to exonerate from liability for the disruption. It should be noted that unlike usual occasions of civil disobedience, there is not here a morally objectionable exercise of authority which confronts the disobedient and which he must meet with defiance in order to provide an opportunity for its objectionability to be legally recognized through legal proceedings based on such acts of defiance. Whatever morally objectionable official conduct there is in the courtroom may be reviewed though appellate procedures other than appeal from a contempt citation. Hence the required attempt at legal vindication would precede any justifiable disruption.

Even when there is no right to defy authority, the conduct of the disrupter may be seen as less offensive because of certain conditions under which he acted or certain circumstances in which the disruption took place. As is the case generally in assessing liability for anti-social conduct, if law is to be morally sound, these grounds of justification or of excuse must play their role in decisions about whether there ought to be liability to punishment and if so in what measure. Certainly some disruptions are, when appreciated in context, so little blameworthy as to be accounted criminally inoffensive, and among the remainder some far less offensive than others. I shall not attempt to set rules for exemption from liability, but only offer what a bit of preliminary spadework turns up.

Very considerable provocation surely results from the inhumane treatment, frustrated expectations, and harassment experienced by criminal defendants during the time of their pretrial detention, and often it would be a deplorable omission in the interest of justice if that is not taken into account. There are two exculpatory views possible. One is that the treatment to which the accused has been subjected tends in some measure to *excuse* his enraged outburst, while the other is that it tends to *justify* protest and resistance.

Then there is the matter of worthiness of motive in genuinely seeking to change a system or protest injustice to oneself or to others. Surely we should want to differentiate between conduct springing from these motives, which may well be thought entitled to some opportunity to assert itself even if disruptive of the proceedings, and conduct stemming from a calculated hostility to authority bereft of goals supportable in principle. Furthermore, innocence of motive is a proper consideration. If we find that the disrupter was concerned to protest rather than to disrupt, even though misguided in his protest, we should count that in his favor in weighing culpability.

Not only motives but conduct itself may be worthy. A plain injustice may have been perpetrated, and the disrupter may have been acting to oppose it by the only means that would be practically effective. This surely is a particularly weighty consideration.

In all these cases we must consider whether motives and intentions are *in fact* what they are said to be. It is not infrequently the case that morally reprehensible disruptive conduct is misrepresented as having been engaged in for worthwhile ends. No mere recitation of polemic formulas confers a degree of immunity on those who wish thereby to gain the benefit of association with legitimate causes.

Incidents of courtroom disruption will have to be sorted and judged in the light of these considerations if justice to the disrupter is to be done. Although we may not expect much in the way of hard rules of law creating rights of justifiable disruption, we may hope for an enlightened exercise of discretionary powers to keep order in the courtroom. And that is something of even greater practical consequence.

Reply

GRAHAM HUGHES

There is much in Gross' response with which I can agree, but there are one or two places where I am not persuaded by his way of putting the matter.

To begin with, I do not see the relevance of his doubts about the appropriateness of the central concept of obedience to law. One can readily agree that for much of the law, which confers powers and sets out conditions for their exercise, the concept of obedience is not the best *entrée* to an analysis. Thus, if the law provides a procedure for making a valid will and, out of stubbornness or negligence, I do not follow it, I just will not have made an effective will; this is much more like ignoring the principles of navigation than disobeying an order. But the theme of my paper was, of course, the disruption of the judicial process, where the application of punitive sanctions is the question at issue, and in such a criminal law context, the concept of obedience would seem to make good sense. To make the point that we are still discussing responses to rules rather than submission to an individual sovereign, we might indeed talk of "compliance" rather than "obedience," but it is not obvious that this relates centrally to the principal issues. Gross himself seems content most of the time to talk about "civil disobedience," as if that were an acceptable characterization of the topic.

Gross proceeds to deny the existence of a *prima facie* obligation to obey the law. This is too large a question to proceed much further with at this point, except to say that I am not persuaded by his argument, which appears to rely exclusively on the *process* by which law is created and to ignore the *function* of law in society. It is the function of law rather than the process of lawmaking which gives rise to the *prima facie* moral obligation. In any event,

Gross' position here does not seem, taken alone, to challenge any of the conclusions I reached in my paper.

Coming to a more particular discussion of some of my examples, Gross observes that "all just and prudent law enforcement is selective." This may be so, but it is clearly not the case that all selective law enforcement is just and prudent. I take it, from his comments, that Gross would in turn agree with this, but that he simply does not view the facts in this context as amounting to a "collapse of the legal system" in any discernible category of law enforcement. We may be in agreement on principle, though this might depend on a fuller discussion of what Gross means by his reference to the "collapse of a legal system" as a necessary condition for the justification of the disruption of the judicial process.

"Harmless Immoralities" and Offensive Nuisances

JOEL FEINBERG

I am not at all sure that there are any private immoral actions that do not cause harm, but I am quite sure that *if* there are such things, there is no justification for their suppression by the state and especially not for their proscription by the criminal law. On the other hand, there clearly are such things as actions that are very offensive to others, and I think the state is justified in preventing at least some of these when certain strict conditions have been satisfied. In coming to these conclusions (which I shall defend in what follows) I appear to have endorsed one and rejected another of the principles commonly proposed as justifications for political restriction of private liberty. Preventing offense, I maintain, is at least sometimes a ground for limiting liberty, whereas the "enforcement of morality as such" is never a valid ground.

I

There are perhaps as many as seven liberty-limiting principles that are frequently proposed by leading writers. It has been held that restriction of a person's liberty may be justified:[1]

1. to prevent injury to others (the *private harm principle*);
2. to prevent impairment of institutional practices and regulatory systems that are in the public interest, such as the collection of taxes and custom duties (the *public harm principle*);

This is an expanded version of the material from Chapters 2 and 3 of *Social Philosophy* by Joel Feinberg, copyright © 1973 by Prentice-Hall, Inc., Englewood Cliffs, N.J. By permission of the publishers.

3. to prevent offense to others (the *offense principle*);
4. to prevent harm to self (*legal paternalism*);[2]
5. to prevent or punish sin, i.e. "to enforce morality as such" (*legal moralism*);
6. to benefit the self (*extreme paternalism*);[3]
7. to benefit others (the *welfare principle*).

The private harm principle, which of course is indissolubly associated with the name of John Stuart Mill, is virtually beyond controversy. Hardly anyone would deny the state the right to make criminal, on this ground, such harmful conduct as willful homicide, aggravated assault, and robbery. Mill often wrote as if the prevention of private harm were the *sole* valid ground for state coercion, but this must surely not have been his considered intention. He would not have wiped from the books such crimes as tax evasion, smuggling, and contempt of court, which need not injure to any measurable degree any assignable individuals, except insofar as they weaken public institutions in whose health we all have a stake, however indirect. I assume then that Mill held both the private and the public versions of the harm principle.

In some sections of *On Liberty*, Mill suggests that harm of one kind or another is the *only* valid ground for coercion, so that the prevention of mere offensiveness, as opposed to harmfulness, can never be sufficient ground to warrant interference with liberty. Yet in the final chapter of *On Liberty*, Mill seems to retreat on this issue too. There he refers to public acts that are "a violation of good manners and, coming thus within the category of offenses against others, may rightly be prohibited. Of this kind," he continues, "are offenses against decency, on which it is unnecessary to dwell. . . ."[4] Mill's view about offensiveness can be made consistent, however, in the following way. One subclass of actions, on his view, has a very special social importance. These actions are instances of expressing orally or in print opinions about matters of fact and about historical, scientific, theological, philosophical, political, and moral questions.[5] The free expression of opinion is of such great importance to the well-being and progress of the community, that

it can be validly restricted only to prevent certain very clear harms
to individuals, such as libel, slander, incited violence, and, perhaps,
invasions of privacy. The importance of free expression is so great
and so special that only the necessity to prevent direct and substantial harm to assignable persons can be a sufficient reason for overriding the presumption in its favor. Mere shock to tender sensibilities can never be a weighty enough harm to counterbalance the
case for free expression of opinion. But Mill did not consider public nudity, indecency, public displays of "dirty pictures," and the
like, to be forms of "symbolic speech," or expressions of *opinion*
of any kind. The presumption in favor of liberty is much weaker
in the case of conduct that does not have the "redeeming social importance" peculiar to assertion, criticism, advocacy, and debate;
and hence, even "mere offensiveness" in the absence of harm may
be a valid ground for suppressing it.[6]

II

What is offensiveness and how is it related to harm? If we follow some legal writers and define "harm" as the violation of an
interest, and then posit a universal interest in not being offended,
it will follow that to suffer offense is to suffer a kind of harm. But
there are some offenses that are (in a narrow sense) "harmless" in
that they do not lead to any *further* harm, that is, they do not violate any interests other than the interest in not being offended.
Thus, there is a sense of "offense" which is contrasted with harm,
and in the interest of clarity, that is the sense we should employ.

Offensive behavior is such in virtue of its capacity to induce in
others any of a large miscellany of mental states that have little in
common except that they are unpleasant, uncomfortable, or disliked. These states do not necessarily "hurt," as sorrow and distress
do. Rather the relation between them and hurt is analogous to that
between physical unpleasantness and pain. There are, after all, a
great variety of unpleasant but not painful bodily states—itches,
shocks, and discomforts—that have little in common except that
they don't hurt but are nevertheless universally disliked.

No complete catalog of the unpleasant states caused by offensiveness is possible here, but surely among the main ones are: irritating sensations (e.g. bad smells and loud noises); unaffected disgust and acute repugnance as caused, for example, by extreme vulgarity and filth; shocked moral, religious, or patriotic sensibilities; unsettling anger or irritation as caused, for example, by another's "obnoxious, insulting, rude, or insolent behavior"; and shameful embarrassment or invaded privacy, as caused, for example, by another's nudity or indecency.

Nuisance law protects people from loud noises, noisome stenches, and other direct and inescapable irritants to the senses, usually by providing civil remedies. An evil smell, of course, even when not harmful (in the narrow sense) can still be an annoyance, inconvenience, or irritation. Something like "unaffected disgust" is often evoked by behavior that is neither harmful nor in any ordinary sense "immoral," but is rather vulgar, uncouth, crass, boorish, or unseemly to an extreme. Normally, bad manners are considered beneath the attention of either morals or law, but when they are bad enough, some have plausibly argued, we can demand "protection" from them. Imagine a filthy and verminous man who scratches himself, spits, wipes his nose with the back of his hand, slobbers, and speaks in a raucous voice uttering mostly profanities and obscenities. If such a person spoke freely to passers-by on the public street, he just might be subject to arrest as a public nuisance, whether he harms anyone or not.

Still other offensive behavior tends to arouse outrage and indignation more than "unaffected disgust." Because the connection between open displays of disapproved conduct and indignation is so well known, engaging in such conduct is frequently a deliberate way of issuing a symbolic insult to a group of people. Sometimes open flaunting is in itself a kind of taunting or challenging and is well understood as "an invitation to violence." The flaunter deliberately arouses shocked anger and revulsion just as if he were saying with contempt, "That's what I think of you and your precious values!" The wearing and displaying of Nazi emblems in

New York would enrage and challenge in this manner. So, alas, would a racially mixed couple strolling harmlessly, hand in hand, down the streets of Jackson, Mississippi. The latter kind of behavior, of course, can have a point and a motive independent of the desire to flaunt and taunt. Engaging in such behavior in public must be known to affront the sensibilities of those regarded as benighted; but its motive may not be to taunt so much as to display one's independence and contempt for custom while boldly affirming, and thus vindicating, one's rights.

When there is no point to the flaunted conduct independent of the desire to offend, still another model is sometimes appropriate, namely, that of desecration or sacrilege. The sacred, whatever else it may be, is no laughing matter. A person to whom "nothing is sacred" is a person able to mock or ridicule anything. But most of us are so constructed that some things are beyond mockery to us. It is difficult then to tolerate swastikas (with their symbolic suggestions of barbarity and genocide) or public flag burnings, or dragging venerated religious symbols in the mud. These things are so widely and intensely resented that some find it hard to think of reasons why they should be tolerated.

Still another kind of offensive behavior is that usually called "indecent." Indecency can have any of the motives and intended effects discussed above. Its distinctive feature is the public exhibition of that which, because of its extremely personal or intimately interpersonal character, had best remain hidden from view, according to prevailing mores. To be offended by indecency is not to be insulted or angered so much as to be acutely and profoundly embarrassed. Indecency, like other offensiveness, may be indirectly harmful when it exacerbates guilt, leads to incapacitating shock, sets a bad example, or provokes violence; but when the law forbids even "harmless indecency," its primary purpose is simply to protect the "unwilling witness of it in the streets."[7]

I have little doubt than that the offense principle should supplement the private and public harm principles in any full statement of the grounds for justifiable constraint. That principle, however, is as dangerous as it is necessary, and, as I shall argue in the section on obscenity below, it must be hedged in with careful qualifications.[8]

III

Are there any harmless immoralities? According to the utilitarian conception of ethics, harmfulness is the very ground and essential nature of immorality; but there is no doubt that our moral code is not (yet) wholly utilitarian. Certain actions are still widely held to be immoral even though they harm no one or, at most, only the actor himself. The question is whether the law should be used to force people to refrain from such conduct.

The central problem cases are those criminal actions generally called morals offenses. Offenses against morality and decency have long constituted a category of crimes (as distinct from offenses against the person, offenses against property, etc.). These have included mainly sex offenses—adultery, fornication, sodomy, incest, and prostitution, but also a miscellany of nonsexual offenses including cruelty to animals, desecration of the flag or other venerated symbols, and mistreatment of corpses. In a very useful article, Louis B. Schwartz maintains that what sets these crimes off as a class is not their special relation to morality (after all, murder is also an offense against morality, but it is not a "morals offense") but rather the lack of an essential connection between them and social harm. In particular, their suppression is not required by the public security.[9] Some morals offenses may harm the perpetrators themselves, but there is rarely harm of this sort the risk of which was not consented to in advance by the actors. Offense to other parties, when it occurs, is a consequence of the perpetration of the offending deeds *in public* and can be prevented by "public nuisance" laws or by statutes against "open lewdness" or "solicitation" in public places. That still leaves "morals offenses" when committed by consenting adults in private: should they really be crimes?

Some arguments in favor of the statutes that create morals offenses are drawn from the private and public harm principles. There might be no direct unconsented-to harm caused by discreet and private, illicit sex relations, it is sometimes conceded; but indirectly harmful consequences to innocent parties or to society itself invariably result. The socially useful institutions of marriage and the family can be weakened, and the chaste life made more difficult. Such indirect and diffuse consequences, however, are highly speculative, and there is no hard evidence that penal laws would prevent them in any case. On the other hand, the harm principles might be used to argue *against* such laws on the grounds that some of the side effects of the laws themselves are invariably harmful. Laws against homosexuality, for example, lead to the iniquities of selective enforcement and to enhanced opportunities for blackmail and private vengeance. Moreover, "the criminal law prevents some deviates from seeking psychiatric aid. Further, the pursuit of homosexuals involves policemen in degrading entrapment practices, and diverts attention and effort that could be employed more usefully against the crimes of violent aggression, fraud, and government corruption, which are the overriding concerns of our metropolitan civilization."[10]

Indeed, the essentially utilitarian argument based on the need for prudent allocation of our social energies in fighting crime may, by itself, be a conclusive argument against the use of the criminal sanction to prevent private (and therefore inoffensive) conduct whose harmfulness is indirect and speculative at most. While seriously harmful crimes against person and property are everywhere on the rise, our police stations, criminal courts, and prisons are flooded with persons charged with drunkenness or marijuana possession, and other perpetrators of "crimes without victims," and if their numbers are not joined by swarms of fornicators, pornographers, and homosexuals, it is only because detection of such "criminals" is so difficult. Only an occasional morals offender is swept into the police nets out of the tens of millions who must violate some part of our sex laws, and these are usually members of economically deprived classes and minority races. Herbert Packer gives sound advice, then, when he cautions the rational legislator that "every dollar and every man-hour is the object of competition among uses," and that "he should not only put first things first, but also, what is perhaps harder, put last things last."[11] From the point of view of resource allocation in the fight against crime, *"merely* moral offenses," that is, those disapproved acts that neither harm nor offend (if there are such) are indeed "last things."

It is another matter to use the criminal law to prevent the offense caused to disgusted captive observers by unavoidable public behavior. In such cases, the offense principle can justify a statute forcing the offending parties to restrict their offensive conduct to private places. This would be to use the law to prevent indecency, however, not immorality as such.[12] Such a statute would be very little more restrictive of liberty than similarly grounded statutes against public nudity. Some conduct may be so offensive as to amount to a kind of "psychic aggression," in which case, the private harm principle would allow its suppression on the same grounds as that of physical assault. But even when all this is said and done, the harm and offense principles together will not support all "enforcement of morality as such," for they do not permit interference with the voluntary conduct of consenting adults in the privacy of their own rooms behind locked doors and drawn blinds.

For these reasons many writers have argued for the repeal of statutes that prohibit private immorality; but not surprisingly the same considerations have led others to abandon the view that the harm and offense principles provide an adequate guide to legislative policy. The alternative principle of "legal moralism" favored by the latter writers has several forms. In its more moderate version, it is commonly associated with the views of Patrick Devlin.[13] Lord Devlin's theory, as I understand it, is really a form of utilitarianism or, more exactly, an application of the public harm principle. The proper aim of the criminal law, he holds, is the prevention of harm, not merely harm to individuals but also, and primarily, harm to society itself. A shared moral code, Devlin argues, is a necessary condition for the very existence of a community. Shared moral convictions function as "invisible bonds" or a kind of "social cement" tying individuals together into an orderly society. Moreover the fundamental unifying morality (to switch the metaphor) is a kind of "seamless web":[14] To damage it at one point is to weaken it throughout. Hence, society has as much right to protect its moral code by legal coercion as it does to protect its equally indispensable political institutions. The law cannot tolerate politically revolutionary activity; nor can it accept activity that rips asunder its moral fabric. Thus, "The suppression of vice is as much the law's business as the suppression of subversive activities; it is no more possible to define a sphere of private morality than it is to define one of private subversive activity."[15]

H. L. A. Hart finds it plausible that some shared morality is necessary to the existence of a community, but criticizes Devlin's further contention "that a society is identical with its morality as that is at any given moment of its history, so that a change in its morality is tantamount to the destruction of a society."[16] Indeed a moral critic might admit that we can't exist as a society without some morality or other, while insisting that we can perfectly well exist without *this* morality (if we put a better one in its place). Devlin seems to reply to this criticism that the shared morality *can* be changed even though protected by law, and when it does change, then the emergent reformed morality in turn deserves *its* legal protection.[17] The law then functions to make moral reform difficult, but there is no preventing change where the reforming zeal is fierce enough. How then does one bring about a change in prevailing moral beliefs when they are enshrined in law? Presumably one advocates conduct which is in fact illegal; one puts into public practice what one preaches; one demonstrates one's sincerity by marching proudly off to jail for one's convictions:

> there is . . . a natural respect for opinions that are sincerely held. When such opinions accumulate enough weight, the law must either yield or it is broken. In a democratic society . . . there will be a strong tendency for it to yield—not to abandon all defenses so as to let in the horde, but to give ground to those who are prepared to fight for something that they prize. To fight may be to suffer. A

willingness to suffer is the most convincing proof of sincerity. Without the law there would be no proof. The law is the anvil on which
the hammer strikes.[18]

In this remarkable passage, Devlin has discovered another argument for enforcing "morality as such," and incidentally for principled civil disobedience as the main technique for initiating and
regulating moral change. A similar argument, deriving from Sam-
uel Johnson, and applying mainly to changes in religious doctrine,
was well known to Mill. Religious innovators deserve to be perse-
cuted, on this theory, for persecution allows them to prove their
mettle and demonstrate their disinterested good faith, while their
teachings, insofar as they are true, cannot be hurt, since truth will
always triumph in the end. Mill regarded this method of testing
truth to be uneconomical, as well as ungenerous:

> To discover to the world something which deeply concerns it, and of
> which it was previously ignorant, to prove to it that it had been mis-
> taken on some vital point of temporal or spiritual interest, is as impor-
> tant a service as a human being can render to his fellow creatures.
> . . . That the authors of such splendid benefits should be requited by
> martyrdom, that their reward should be to be dealt with as the vilest
> of criminals, is not, upon this theory, a deplorable error and misfor-
> tune for which humanity should mourn in sackcloth and ashes, but the
> normal and justifiable state of things. . . . People who defend this
> mode of treating benefactors cannot be supposed to set much value
> on the benefit.[19]

If self-sacrificing civil disobedience, on the other hand, is not the
most efficient and humane remedy to grant to the moral reformer,
what instruments of moral change are available for him? This question is not only difficult to answer in its own right, it is also the
rock that sinks Devlin's favorite analogy between harmless immorality and political subversion.

Consider what subversion is. In most modern law-governed
countries there is a constitution, a set of duly constituted authorities, and a body of statutes, or "positive laws," created and enforced by the duly constituted authorities. There will be ways of
changing these things that are well known, orderly, and permitted

by the constitution. For example, constitutions are amended; new legislation is introduced; legislators are elected. On the other hand, it is easy to conceive of various sorts of unpermitted and disorderly change, for example, through assassination and violent revolution, or through bribery and subornation, or through the use of legitimately won power to extort and intimidate. Only these illegitimate methods of change, of course, can be called "subversion." But here the analogy between positive law and positive morality begins to break down. There is no "moral constitution," no well-known and orderly way of introducing moral legislation to duly constituted moral legislators, no clear convention of majority rule. Moral subversion, if there is such a thing, must consist in the employment of disallowed techniques of change instead of the officially permitted "constitutional" ones. It consists not simply of change as such, but of illegitimate change. Insofar as the notion of legitimately induced moral change remains obscure, "illegitimate moral change" can do no better. Still, there is enough content to both notions to preserve some analogy to the political case. A citizen works *legitimately* to change prevailing moral beliefs when he publicly and forthrightly expresses his own dissent; when he attempts to argue, and persuade, and offer reasons; when he lives according to his own convictions with persuasive quiet and dignity, neither harming others nor offering counterpersuasive offense to tender sensibilities. On the other hand, a citizen attempts to change mores by *illegitimate* means when he abandons argument and example for force and fraud. If this is the basis of the distinction between legitimate and illegitimate techniques of moral change, then the use of state power to affect moral belief *one way or the other*, when harmfulness is not involved, would be a clear example of illegitimacy. Government enforcement of the conventional code is not to be called "moral subversion," of course, because it is used on behalf of the *status quo*; but whether conservative or innovative it is equally in defiance of our "moral constitution"—if anything is.

The second version of legal moralism is the pure version, not some other principle in disguise, but legal moralism properly so called. The enforcement of morality as such and the attendant punishment of sin are not justified as means to some further social aim (such as the preservation of social cohesiveness) but are ends in themselves. Perhaps J. F. Stephen was expressing this pure moralism when he wrote that "there are acts of wickedness so gross and outrageous that self-protection apart they must be prevented at any cost to the offender and punished if they occur with exemplary severity."[20] (From his examples it is clear that Stephen had in mind the very acts that are called "morals offenses" in the law.) That the act to be punished is truly wicked and outrageous must be the virtually unanimous opinion of society, Stephen goes on to add; and the public condemnation of acts of its kind must be "strenuous and unequivocal."[21]

Adequate discussion of Stephen's view requires that a distinction be made between the moral code actually in existence at a given time and place, and some ideal rational code. The former is often called "conventional" or "positive" morality, and the latter "rational" or "critical" morality. Whether or not a given type of act is wicked according to a given positive morality is a matter of sociological fact; whether or not it is "truly wicked" is a question for argument of a different kind and notoriously more difficult to settle. Stephen apparently identified critical morality in large measure with the Victorian positive morality of his time and place. A century later we can be pardoned, I think, for being somewhat skeptical about that. Once we grant that there is no necessary and self-evident correspondence between some given positive morality and the true critical morality, it becomes plain that the pure version of legal moralism is one or another of two distinct principles, depending on which sense of "morality" it employs.

Consider first, then, the view that the legal enforcement of positive morality is an end in itself. This means that it is good for its own sake that the state prohibit and punish all actions of a kind held wicked by the vast majority of citizens, even when such acts are harmless and done in private with all deference to the moral sensibilities of others. It is hard to argue against propositions that derive their support mainly from ethical intuition, but when one fully grasps the concept of a *positive morality*, even the intuitive basis of this moralistic proposition begins to dissolve. What is so precious, one wonders, about public opinion as such? Let us suppose that public opinion about moral questions is wrong, as it so often has been in the past. Is there still some intrinsic value in its legal enforcement derived from the mere fact that it *is* public opinion? This hardly seems plausible, much less intuitively certain, especially when one considers that enforcement would make it all the more difficult to correct the mistake. Perhaps it gives the public some satisfaction to know that conduct it regards (rightly or wrongly) as odious or sinful occurs very rarely even behind drawn blinds and that when it occurs, it is punished with "exemplary severity." But again it is hard to see how such "satisfaction" could have any intrinsic value; and even if we grant it intrinsic value for the sake of the argument, we should have to weigh it against such solid intrinsic evils as the infliction of suffering and the invasion of privacy.

The more plausible version of pure moralism restricts its scope to critical morality. This is the view that the state is justified in enforcing a truly rational morality as such and in punishing deviations from that morality even when they are of a kind that is not harmful to others. This principle too is said to rest on an intuitive basis. It is often said that the universe is an intrinsically worse place for having immoral (even harmlessly immoral) conduct in it. The threat of punishment (the argument continues) deters such conduct. The actual instances of punishment not only back up the threat, and thus help keep future moral weeds out of the universe's garden, they also erase the past evils from the universe's temporal record by "nullifying" them, or making it as if they never were. Thus punishment contributes to the net intrinsic value of the universe in two ways: by cancelling out past sins and preventing future ones.[22]

There may be some minimal plausibility in this view when it is applied to ordinary harmful crimes, especially those involving duplicity or cruelty, which really do seem to "set the universe out of joint." It is natural enough to think of repentance, apology, or forgiveness as "setting things straight," and of punishment as a kind of "payment" or a wiping clean of the moral slate. But in cases where it is natural to resort to such analogies, there is not only a rule infraction, there is also a *victim*—some person or society of persons who have been harmed. When there is no victim—and especially where there is no profit at the expense of another—"setting things straight" has no clear intuitive content.

Punishment may yet play its role in discouraging harmless private immoralities for the sake of "the universe's moral record." But if fear of punishment is to keep people from illicit intercourse (or from desecrating flags or mistreating corpses) in the privacy of their own rooms, then morality must be enforced with a fearsome efficiency that shows no respect for anyone's privacy. There may be some, like Stephen, who would derive great satisfaction from the thought that no harmless immoralities are being perpetrated behind anyone's locked doors (to the greater credit of the universe as a whole); but how many of these would be willing to sacrifice their *own* privacy for this "satisfaction"? Yet if private immoralities are to be deterred by threat of punishment, the detecting authorities *must* be able to look, somehow, into the hidden chambers and locked rooms of anyone's private domicile. And when we put this massive forfeiture of privacy into the balance along with the usual costs of coercion—loss of spontaneity, stunting of rational powers, anxiety, hypocrisy, and the rest—the price of securing mere outward conformity to the community's moral standards (for that is all that can be achieved by the penal law) is exorbitant.

In an extremely acute article,[23] Ronald Dworkin suggests (without fully endorsing) a version of pure legal moralism that shares some of the features of both versions discussed above. He distinguishes between genuine moral convictions and mere prejudices, personal aversions, arbitrary dogmas, and rationalizations. The actual moral convictions of a community, providing they constitute a genuine "discriminatory morality," Dworkin suggests, might well be enforced by the criminal law; but the "morality" that consists in mere emotional aversion, no matter how widespread, is a morality only in a weak "anthropological sense" and is undeserving of legal enforcement. Indeed, "the belief that prejudices, personal aversions, and rationalizations do not justify restricting another's freedom itself occupies a critical and fundamental position in our popular morality."[24] The consensus judgment in our community that homosexuality is wicked, in Dworkin's view, is not a genuine moral judgment at all, and "what is shocking and wrong is not [Devlin's] idea that the community's morality counts, but his idea of what counts as the community's morality."[25]

Dworkin's point is a good one against Devlin's position on sexual offenses, but I would go much further still. Even if there is a *genuine* moral consensus in a community that certain sorts of "harmless" activities are wrong, I see no reason why that consensus should be enforced by the criminal law and at least one very good reason why it ought not to be enforced: even a genuine "discriminatory" popular morality might, for all of that, be *mistaken*, and legal enforcement inhibits critical dissent and prevents progressive improvement.

Among the nonsexual morals offenses, cruelty to animals is the most interesting hard case for the application of liberty-limiting principles. Suppose that John Doe is an intelligent, sensitive person with one very neurotic trait—he loves to see living things suffer pain. Fortunately, he never has occasion to torture human beings (he would genuinely regret that) for he can always find an animal for the purpose. For a period he locks himself in his room every night, carefully draws the blind, and then beats and tortures a dog to death. The sounds of shrieks and moans, which are music to his ears, are nuisances however to his neighbors; and when his landlady discovers what he has been doing, she is so shocked she has to be hospitalized. Distressed that he has caused harm to human beings, Doe leaves the rooming house, buys a five-hundred acre ranch, and moves into a house in the remote unpopulated center of his own property. There in the perfect privacy of his own home, he spends every evening maiming, torturing, and beating to death his own animals.

What are we to say of Doe's bizarre behavior? We have three alternatives. First we can say that it is perfectly permissible consisting as it does simply in a man's destruction of his own property. How a man disposes in private of his own property is no concern of anyone else providing he causes no nuisance such as loud noises and evil smells. Second, we can say that this behavior is patently immoral even though it causes no harm to the interests of anyone other than the actor; and further, since it obviously should not be permitted by the law, that this is a case where the harm and offense principles are inadequate and must be supplemented by legal moralism. Third, we can extend the harm principle to animals and argue that the law can interfere with the private enjoyment of property in this case not to enforce "morality as such" but rather to prevent harm to the animals. The third alternative is the most inviting, but it is not without its difficulties. We *must* control animal movements, exploit animal labor, and in many cases, deliberately slaughter animals. All these forms of treatment would be "harm" if inflicted on human beings, but cannot be allowed to count as harm to animals if the harm principle is to be extended to animals in a realistic way. The best compromise is to recognize one supreme interest of animals, namely the interest in freedom from cruelly or wantonly inflicted pain, and to count as "harm" all and only invasions of *that* interest.

IV

Up to this point we have considered the harm and offense principles together in order to determine whether between them they are sufficient to regulate conventional immoralities, or whether they need help from some further independent principle (legal moralism). Morals offenses were treated as essentially private so that the offense principle could not be stretched to apply to them. Obscene literature is quite different in this respect. It is material deliberately published for the eyes of others, and its existence can bring partisans of the unsupplemented harm and offense principles into head-on conflict.

"Obscenity" has both an ordinary and a technical legal sense. In the untechnical pre-legal sense, it refers to material dealing with nudity, sex, or excretion in an offensive manner. Such material becomes obscene in the legal sense when either because of its offensiveness or for some other reason (this question had best be left open in the definition), it is or ought to be without legal protection. The legal sense then incorporates the everyday one, and essential to both is the requirement that the material be *offensive*. One and the same item may offend one person and not another. "Obscenity," if it is to avoid this subjective relativity, must involve an interpersonal objective sense of "offensive." For material to be offensive in the requisite sense it must be so by prevailing community standards that are public and well known, or be such that it is apt to offend virtually everyone.

The American Civil Liberties Union, adopting an approach characteristic of both the friends and the foes of censorship in an earlier period, insists that the offensiveness of obscenity is much too trivial a ground to warrant prior restraint or censorship.[26] The A.C.L.U. argument for this position treats literature, drama, and painting as forms of expression subject to the same rules as expressions of opinion. The power to censor and punish, it maintains, involves risks of great magnitude that socially valuable material will be repressed along with the "filth"; and the overall effect of suppression, it insists, can only be to discourage nonconformist and eccentric expression generally. In order to override these serious risks, the A.C.L.U. concludes, there must be in a given case an even more clear and present danger that the obscene material, if not squelched, will cause even greater harm; and evidence of this countervailing kind is never forthcoming (especially when "mere offense" is not counted as a kind of harm).

The A.C.L.U. stand on obscenity seems clearly to be the position dictated by the unsupplemented harm principles and their corollary, the clear and present danger test. Is there any reason at this point to introduce the offense principle into the discussion? Unhappily, we may be forced to do just that if we are to do justice to all of our particular intuitions in the most harmonious way. Consider an example suggested by Louis B. Schwartz. By the provisions of the new Model Penal Code, he writes, "a rich homosexual may not use a billboard on Times Square to promulgate to the general populace the techniques and pleasures of sodomy."[27] If the notion of "harm" is restricted to its narrow sense that is contrasted with "offense," it will be hard to reconstruct a rationale for this prohibition that is based on a harm principle. It is unlikely that there would be evidence that a lurid and obscene public poster in Times Square would create a clear and present danger of injury to those unfortunate persons who fail to avert their eyes in time as they come blinking out of the subway stations. And yet it will be surpassingly difficult even for the most dedicated liberal to advocate freedom of expression in a case of this kind. Hence, if we are to justify coercion in this case, we will likely be driven, however reluctantly, to the offense principle.

There is good reason to be "reluctant" to embrace the offense principle until driven to it by an example of the above kind. People take offense—perfectly genuine offense—at many socially useful or harmless activities, from commercial advertisements to inane chatter. Moreover, as we have seen, irrational prejudices of a very widespread kind can lead people to be disgusted, shocked, even morally repelled by perfectly innocent activities, and we should be loath to permit their groundless repugnance to override the innocence. The offense principle, therefore, must be formulated in a very precise way so as not to open the door to wholesale and intuitively unwarranted repression.

It is instructive to note that a strictly drawn offense principle would not only justify prohibition of public conduct and publicly pictured conduct that is in its inherent character repellent (e.g., buggery, bestiality, sexual sado-masochism), but also conduct and pictured conduct that is inoffensive in itself but offensive only when it occurs in inappropriate circumstances. I have in mind so-called indecencies such as public nudity. One can imagine an advocate of the harm principle more extreme (and perhaps more consistent) even than J. S. Mill who argues against the public nudity prohibition on the grounds that the sight of a naked body does no one any harm and that the state has no right to impose any given standards of dress or undress on private citizens. How one chooses to dress, after all, is a form of self-expression. If we do not permit the state to bar clashing colors, or bizarre hair styles, by what right does it prohibit total undress? Perhaps the sight of naked people could lead to riots or other forms of anti-social behavior, but that is precisely the sort of contingency for which we have police. If we don't take away a man's right of free speech for the reason that its exercise may lead others to misbehave, we cannot in consistency deny his right to dress or undress as he chooses for the same reason.

There may be no answering this challenge on its own ground; but the offense principle provides a special rationale of its own for the nudity prohibition. There is no doubt that the sight of nude bodies in public places is for almost everyone acutely *embarrassing*. Part of the explanation, no doubt, rests on the fact that nudity has an irresistible power to draw the eye and focus the thoughts on matters that are normally repressed. The conflict between these attracting and repressing forces, between allure and disgust,[28] is exciting, upsetting, and anxiety-producing. In most persons it will create a kind of painful turmoil at best and at worst, that experience of exposure to oneself of one's "peculiarly sensitive, intimate, vulnerable aspects"[29] which is called *shame*. When one has not been able to prepare one's defenses, "one's feeling is involuntarily exposed openly in one's face. . . . We are . . . caught unawares, made a fool of."[30] For many people the result is not mere "offense," but a kind of psychic jolt that can be a painful wound. Those better able to cope with their feelings might well resent the necessity to do so and regard it as an irritating distraction and a bore, much the same as any other nuisance.[31]

V

If we are to accept the offense principle as a supplement to the harm principles, we must accept two mediating norms of interpretation which stand to it in a way similar to that in which the clear and present danger test stands to the harm principles. The first is the *standard of universality* which has already been touched upon. The interracial couple strolling hand in hand down the streets of Jackson, Mississippi, without question cause shock and mortification, even shame and disgust, to the overwhelming majority of white pedestrians who happen to observe them; but we surely don't want our offense principle applied to justify preventive coercion on that ground. To avoid that consequence let us stipulate that in order for "offense" (repugnance, embarrassment, shame, etc.) to be sufficient to warrant coercion, it should be the reaction that could reasonably be expected from almost any person chosen at random, taking the nation as a whole, and not because the individual selected belongs to some faction, clique, or party.

That qualification should be more than sufficient to protect the interracial couple, but, alas, it may yield undesirable consequences in another class of cases. I have in mind abusive, mocking, insulting behavior or speech attacking specific subgroups of the population—especially ethnic, racial, or religious groups. Public cross-burnings, displays of swastikas, "jokes" that ridicule Americans of Polish descent told on public media, public displays of banners with large and abusive caricatures of the Pope[32] are extremely offensive to the groups so insulted, and no doubt also offensive to large numbers of sympathetic outsiders. But still, there will be many millions of people who will not respond emotionally at all, and many millions more who may secretly approve. Thus, our amended offense principle will not justify the criminal proscription of such speech or conduct. I am inclined, therefore, simply to patch up that principle in an *ad hoc* fashion once more. For that special class of offensive behavior (only one of several distinct kinds of offensiveness distinguished in Part II above) that consists in the flaunting of abusive, mocking, insulting behavior of a sort bound to upset, alarm, anger, or irritate those it insults, I would allow the offense principle to apply, even though the behavior would *not* offend the entire population. Those who are taunted by such conduct will understandably suffer intense and complicated emotions. They might be frightened or wounded; and their blood might boil in wrath. Yet the law cannot permit them to accept the challenge and vent their anger in retaliatory aggression. But again, having to cope with one's rage is as burdensome a bore as having to suffer shame, or disgust, or noisome stenches, and the law might well undertake to protect those who are vulnerable, even if they are—indeed, precisely because they are—a minority.[33]

The second mediating principle for the application of the offense principle is the standard of reasonable avoidability. No one has a right to protection from the state against offensive experiences if he can easily and effectively avoid those experiences with no unreasonable effort or inconvenience. If a nude person enters a public bus and takes a seat near the front, there may be no effective way whatever for the other patrons to avoid intensely shameful embarrassment (or other insupportable feelings) short of leaving the bus themselves, which would be an unreasonable inconvenience. Similarly, obscene remarks over a loudspeaker, homosexual billboards in Times Square, pornographic handbills thrust into the hands of passing pedestrians all fail to be reasonably avoidable.

On the other hand, the offense principle, properly qualified, can give no warrant to the suppression of *books* on the grounds of obscenity. When printed words hide decorously behind covers of books sitting passively on the shelves of a bookstore, their offensiveness is easily avoided. The contrary view is no doubt encouraged by the common comparison of obscenity with "smut," "filth," or "dirt." This in turn suggests an analogy to nuisance law, which governs cases where certain activities create loud noises or terrible odors offensive to neighbors, and "the courts must weigh the gravity of the nuisance [substitute "offense"] to the neighbors against the social utility [substitute "redeeming social value"] of the defendant's conduct."[34] There is, however, one vitiating disanalogy in this comparison. In the case of "dirty books," the offense is easily avoidable. There is nothing like the evil smell of rancid garbage oozing right out through the covers of a book whether one looks at it or not. When an "obscene" book sits on a shelf, who is there to be offended? Those who want to read it for the sake of erotic stimulation presumably will not be offended (else they wouldn't read it), and those who choose not to read it will have no experience of it to be offended by. If its covers are too decorous, some innocents may browse through it by mistake and then be offended by what they find, but they need only close the book again to escape the offense. Even this offense, minimal as it is, could be completely avoided by a prior consulting of trusted book reviewers. Moreover, no one forces a customer to browse randomly, and if he is informed in advance of the risk of risqué passages, he should be prepared to shoulder that risk himself without complaint. I conclude that there are no sufficient grounds derived either from the harm or offense principles for suppressing obscene literature, unless that ground be the protection of children; but I see no reason why selective prohibitions for children could not work as well in the case of books as in the cases of cigarettes and whiskey.

Two further restrictions on the offense principle are necessary. The first is implicit in the universality principle but is important enough to be made fully explicit and emphatic. In applying the offense principle, no respect should be shown for *abnormal susceptibilities*. Here again the law of nuisance provides a fitting model. In one typical tort case, for example, the court ruled that "it is not a nuisance to ring a church bell merely because it throws a hypersensitive individual into convulsions."[35] In deciding what kind of conduct is sufficiently annoying to qualify as a nuisance, says Prosser, "some other standard must obviously be adopted than the personal tastes, susceptibilities, and idiosyncrasies of the particular plaintiff. The standard must necessarily be that of definite offensiveness or annoyance to *the normal person in the community.*"[36]

A similar standard in the criminal law would protect us all from homosexual billboards in Times Square, but not from billboard pictures of fully clothed heterosexual lovers. There is one kind of offended sensibility that can certainly not satisfy such a standard, namely the shock or disappointment occasioned by the bare knowledge (no pun intended) that other persons are, or may be, doing immoral things in private. The offense principle cannot be used as a life-raft to save the shipwrecked legal moralist. It is conceivable, I suppose, that there be a person whose moral sensibilities are so tender that bare knowledge of the existence of private "harmless immoralities" would lead to severe mental distress; but in such a case, it would be more plausible to attribute the distress to abnormal susceptibilities than to the precipitating cause. If a sneeze causes a glass window to break, we should blame the weakness or brittleness of the glass and not the sneeze. The offense principle is not different from the private harm principle in this respect: the application of both requires some conception of *normalcy*. It is the person of normal vulnerability whose interests are to be protected by coercive power; the person who, figuratively speaking, can be blown over by a sneeze, cannot demand that other people's vigorous but *normally* harmless activities be suspended by government power for his protection. He can demand protection only against conduct that would harm or offend the normal person in his position. The further protection he needs he must provide for himself—and of course he must be *permitted* to provide for himself—by noncoercive methods.[37]

The final condition for the safe use of the offense principle is that the person constrained by the law from being offensive to others must be granted an allowable alternative outlet or mode of expression, perhaps on analogy with temporary restrictions on free speech based on anti-littering statutes, public expense, or public inconvenience. The public interest in clean streets, perhaps, can justify a municipal restraining order against the distribution of political handbills, but the restraint obviously goes too far if it prevents handouts even by persons willing themselves to clean up the debris or pay for the job, or if it prevents mailings of handbills, and all other modes of dissemination. Similarly, an exhibition of naked love-making or its depiction on the city streets can be banned by the offense principle, but the restraint goes too far if it prevents the same conduct or represented conduct from being shown in a private home or rented theatre to an eager and willing voluntary audience. The offense principle cannot justify the prohibition of "offensive" conduct even where it does not offend, without undergoing metamorphosis into the unpalatable principle of legal moralism.

NOTES

1. I use the word "justified" in the formulation of these principles in such a way that it does not follow from the fact that a given limitation on liberty is justified that the state has a duty to impose it, but only that the state *may* interfere on the ground in question if it should choose to do so. Cf. Ted Honderich, *Punishment: Its Supposed Justifications* (Hutchinson of London, 1969), p. 175. Moreover, as these principles are formulated here, they state sufficient but not necessary conditions for "justified" (that is, permissible) coercion. Each states that interference is permissible *if* (but not *only if*) a certain condition is satisfied. Hence the principles are not mutually exclusive; it is possible to hold two or more of them at once, even all of them together. And it is possible to deny all of them. In fact, since all combinations and permutations of these principles are (logically) possible, there are 2^7 or 128 possible positions (and more) about the legitimacy of coercion represented by the list.

2. For recent detailed discussions of the principle of legal paternalism, see Gerald Dworkin, "Paternalism" in *Morality and the Law*, ed. Richard Wasserstrom (Belmont, Cal.: Wadsworth, 1971), and Joel Feinberg, "Legal Paternalism," *Canadian Journal of Philosophy* 1 (1971): 105–24.

3. I shall not discuss the merits and defects of extreme paternalism and the welfare principle in this paper. Both principles presuppose that sense can be made out of the difficult distinctions between benefitting and not harming, and harming and not benefitting.

4. J. S. Mill, *On Liberty*, Chapter 5, paragraph 7.

5. These are the matters discussed collectively under the rubric "Of the Liberty of Thought and Discussion" in Chapter II of *On Liberty*. As Harry Kalven points out, Mill neglects to include "the novel, the poem, the painting, the drama, or the piece of sculpture" among those expressions that have an extreme social value. The emphasis in Mill, as in Chafee and Meiklejohn, is "all on truth winning out in a fair fight between competing ideas." See Kalven's "Metaphysics of the Law of Obscenity," in

1960: The Supreme Court Review, ed. Philip B. Kurland (Chicago: University of Chicago Press, 1960), pp. 15–16.

6. Mill's view, then, as I have interpreted it, is strikingly similar to that expressed in the majority opinion by Mr. Justice Brennan in *United States vs. Roth* (1957) except that the latter has a conception of "social value" broad enough to include works of art.

7. H. L. A. Hart, *Law, Liberty, and Morality* (Stanford, Cal.: Stanford University Press, 1963), p. 45.

8. Traditionally, offensiveness has tended to arouse even more extreme penalties than harmfulness. The New York Penal Law, for example, until recently provided a maximum sentence of ten years for first degree assault and twenty years for sodomy; Pennsylvania's Penal Code provides a maximum of seven years for assault with intent to kill and ten years for pandering; California provides a maximum of two years for corporal injury to wife or child but fifteen years for "perversion." Mayhem and assault with intent to commit a serious felony get fourteen and twenty years, respectively, in California, but statutory rape and incest get fifty years each. Zechariah Chafee gives the best example I know of perverse judicial zeal to avenge mere offense: "The white slave traffic was first exposed by W. T. Stead in a magazine article, 'The Maiden Tribute.' The English law did absolutely nothing to the profiteers in vice, but put Stead in prison for a year for writing about an indecent subject" (Z. Chafee, *Free Speech in the United States* [Cambridge, Mass.: Harvard University Press, 1964], p. 151). It is worth noting, finally, that the most common generic synonym for "crimes" is neither "harms" nor "injuries," but "offenses."

9. For example, "One has only to stroll along certain streets in Amsterdam to see that prostitution may be permitted to flourish openly without impairing personal security, economic prosperity, or indeed the general moral tone of a most respected nation of the Western world" (Louis B. Schwartz, "Morals Offenses and the Model Penal Code," *Columbia Law Review* 63 [1963]: 670).

10. *Ibid.*, p. 672.

11. Herbert Packer, *The Limits of the Criminal Sanction* (Stanford, Cal.: Stanford University Press, 1968), p. 260.

12. The distinction between immorality and indecency is well put by H. L. A. Hart: "Sexual intercourse between husband and wife is not immoral, but if it takes place in public, it is an affront to public decency. Homosexual intercourse between consenting adults in private is immoral according to conventional morality, but not an affront to public decency, though it would be if it took place in public" (*Law, Liberty, and Morality*, p. 44).

13. Patrick Devlin, *The Enforcement of Morals* (London: Oxford University Press, 1965).

14. The phrase is not Devlin's but rather that of his critic, H. L. A.

Hart, in *Law, Liberty, and Morality*, p. 51. In his rejoinder to Hart, Devlin writes: "Seamlessness presses the simile rather hard, but apart from that, I should say that for most people morality is a web of beliefs, rather than a number of unconnected ones" (Devlin, *Enforcement*, p. 115).

15. Devlin, *Enforcement*, pp. 13–14.
16. Hart, *Law, Liberty, and Morality*, p. 51.
17. Devlin, *Enforcement*, pp. 115ff.
18. *Ibid.*, p. 116.
19. Mill, *On Liberty*, Chapter 2, paragraph 14.
20. James Fitzjames Stephen, *Liberty, Equality, Fraternity* (London, 1873), p. 163.
21. *Ibid.*, p. 159.
22. Cf. C. D. Broad, "Certain Features in Moore's Ethical Doctrines," in *The Philosophy of G. E. Moore*, ed. P. A. Schilpp, (Evanston: Northwestern University Press, 1942), pp. 48ff.
23. Ronald Dworkin, "Lord Devlin and the Enforcement of Morals," *Yale Law Journal*, 75 (1966).
24. *Ibid.*, p. 1001.
25. *Loc. cit.*
26. "Obscenity and Censorship" (New York: American Civil Liberties Union, March, 1963). The approach that was characteristic of the late fifties and early sixties was to assimilate the obscenity question to developed free speech doctrine requiring a showing of a "clear and present danger" of substantive harm to justify government suppression. Obscene materials pertaining to sex (but not excretion!) were taken to be dangerous, if at all, because they are *alluring* and thus capable of tempting persons into antisocial (harmful) conduct. As Herbert Packer points out (*Limits of Criminal Sanction*, p. 319) the clear and present danger test is virtually certain to be passed by even the most offensive materials. Of proposals made in the fifties that such a test be used, he writes: "It is difficult to know whether these suggestions were advanced seriously or tongue in cheek. It seems clear that, conscientiously applied, they would lead to exoneration in all but the most bizarre cases. I prefer to regard them as, in effect, calling the bluff of proponents of the traditional tests. 'If you really are concerned with dangerous tendencies rather than with immorality as such, then put up or shut up.' " In most cases, as it turned out, the arch enemies of obscenity were indeed concerned with "immorality as such." Even the Model Penal Code rule that so influenced the U.S. Supreme Court in the famous *Roth* and *Ginsburg* decisions seems to imply that the existence of sexual thoughts of a "prurient" kind is an inherent evil, and appeal to "prurient interests" a form of wickedness, apart from consequences.
27. Schwartz, "Morals Offenses," p. 681.
28. Use of the word "filthy" to express disgust and revulsion at vulgar treatments of sexual matters, according to Harry Kalven, "points to an

evil of obscenity which is the exact opposite of that usually recognized: the obscene is bad because it is revolting, not because it is alluring." Kalven then goes on to chide the courts for an apparent inconsistency: "Since it [obscenity] cannot be both [revolting and alluring] at the same time for the same audience, it would be well to have more explicit guidance as to which objection controls." Kalven here misses the most important (and elusive) point about obscenity: it *can* be both alluring and revolting at the same time to the same person. Attraction and disgust are often both involved in the complex mechanism of shameful embarrassment, the most distinctive mode of offensiveness produced by obscenity. The quotations are from Kalven's otherwise excellent and very helpful article, "The Metaphysics of the Law of Obscenity," pp. 41–42.

29. Helen Lynd, *On Shame and the Search for Identity* (New York: Science Editions, 1961), p. 33.

30. *Ibid.*, p. 32.

31. There are, of course, those who apparently *enjoy* the tension between allure and disgust, who find its inner turmoil and excitement "thrilling" and actively seek it out, very much as youngsters seek out roller coasters and other exciting rides at amusement parks for the thrill of sensations that are normally alarming and generally taken to be disagreeable. The analogy, I think, is close. In both cases, persons should be permitted to seek and "enjoy" the thrilling sensations, but no person should ever have such sensations imposed upon him without his consent.

32. For a penetrating discussion of an actual case of this description see Zechariah Chafee, *Free Speech in the United States* (Cambridge, Mass.: Harvard University Press, 1964), p. 161.

33. As indeed the laws in many states do. Section 722 of the New York Penal Law, for example, specifies punishment for "disorderly, threatening, insulting language or behavior in public places, and acts which annoy, obstruct, or are offensive to others." A showing of a clear and present danger of substantive harm is presumably not required. In 1939, in a typical prosecution, one Ninfo, a Christian Front street orator, was convicted under this statute for saying "If I had my way, I would hang all the Jews in this country. I wish I had $100,000 from Hitler. I would show those damn Jews what I would do, you mockies, you damn Jews, you scum." See David Riesman, "Democracy and Defamation: Control of Group Libel," *Columbia Law Review*, 42 (1942): 751ff. Reisman discusses not only offensive insults to groups, but the more complex question of group defamation.

34. William L. Prosser, *Handbook of the Law of Torts* (St. Paul: West Publishing Co., 1955).

35. *Rogers v. Elliott* (Massachusetts, 1888).

36. Prosser, *Handbook*, pp. 395–96. Emphasis added.

37. On the other hand, the abnormally vulnerable person should be protected from deliberate and malicious attempts to seek him out, pursue and harass him, and exploit his vulnerability for no respectable purpose.

Comments: Offensive Conduct and the Law

MICHAEL D. BAYLES

Feinberg's paper is an impressive *tour de force*. He clearly and thoroughly analyzes the issues involved, concisely and cogently rejects alternative positions, then persuasively defends a severely restricted principle prohibiting offensive conduct. In so doing he has occupied a quite reasonable, appealing, and thoroughly liberal position. The paper markedly advances discussion of the issues. Many of his conclusions are quite acceptable. Hence, the following comments indicate disagreement with his approach more than with his substantive conclusions.

I

Feinberg begins by presenting seven liberty-limiting principles which have been discussed by various writers, e.g., the private harm principle which states that a person's liberty may be limited to prevent injury to others. These principles, he asserts, only present conditions in which "the state may interfere . . . if it should choose to do so." The principles do not state necessary conditions for state interference, only sufficient ones for " 'justified' (that is, permissible) coercion. Each states that interference is permissible *if* (but not *only if*) a certain condition is satisfied."[1]

Unfortunately, in practice Feinberg does not always follow this account of liberty-limiting principles. First, he claims "the harm principles might be used to argue *against*" some laws. But if the harm principles, as liberty-limiting principles, only present sufficient conditions for permissible state interference, they cannot be used to argue against legislation unless, perhaps, they justify constitutional limitations on law-making. Second, Feinberg's definition of liberty-limiting principles implies that no other principles besides acceptable liberty-limiting ones pertain to justifying legislation; the only other relevant factor is the choice of society. However, he also brings in Herbert Packer's principle of resource allocation, that first things be put first and last things last.[2] Perhaps, like Packer, Feinberg considers the principle of resource allocation one of prudence and not morality. That is, the problem of social priorities is not a moral problem.

Moreover, treating liberty-limiting principles as merely establishing the permissibility of legislation results in a curious gap in arguments for legislation. For no matter how much conduct may harm, offend, or benefit others or the actor, a legislator still does not have a sufficient reason for liberty-limiting legislation. For example, all that arguments from the private harm principle can do is show that legislation is permissible, they do not answer a legislator's question of whether he should vote "aye" or "nay." It is difficult to conceive what other sorts of reasons are needed to answer a legislator's question. If harm, offense, or benefit to people do not provide sufficient reasons for legislation, what else can conceivably do so?

An alternative account of liberty-limiting principles may present issues more clearly and be less cumbersome than Feinberg's. It is not clear whether Feinberg treats only criminal laws as limiting liberty or not. Probably he does not, but all the conduct he discusses in this paper is of the sort which has traditionally been the subject of criminal legislation. Feinberg implicitly recognizes a general presumption against limiting liberty. So long as freedom of choice or action has value, liberty-limiting legislation involves a disvalue. But if liberty is limited by criminal legislation, an even stronger presumption against legislation exists. For those who are found guilty of violating the law suffer a further evil than merely not being free to act as they choose, they are also deprived of other liberties or property, i.e., punished. Hence, reasons for criminal legislation must overcome a stronger presumption against it than must those for noncriminal legislation.

An acceptable principle for liberty-limiting legislation states a condition which constitutes a good reason, but neither a necessary nor a sufficient one, for legislation. The condition in a principle, e.g., offensiveness, is not necessary because the condition in another principle, e.g., harm to others, may by itself justify legislation. It is not a sufficient condition because it might not, in a particular instance, outweigh the presumption against criminal legislation. Also, besides the general presumption, there are other principles that may pertain and state reasons against legislation, e.g., that a law could not be effectively enforced or that it invades privacy. When principles for and against legislation apply to a proposed law, they must be balanced against one another.[3] Collectively, all the principles for and against legislation present a standard of good legislation. Disputes as to which principles are acceptable are disputes as to what constitutes morally good reasons for or against legislation.

II

Feinberg adopts a carefully restricted offense principle. The state has a good reason for limiting liberty if one's conduct causes offense to others provided it would offend a normal member of society, people cannot reasonably avoid the offense, and one is allowed an alternative outlet or mode of expression. Presumably this offense principle can justify criminal legislation since all the limitations of liberty Feinberg advocates may be found in the Model Penal Code. The only feature common to offensive conduct which he finds is that it causes "unpleasant, uncomfortable, or disliked" mental states. He then lists five mental states which are characteristic, if not exhaustive, of offense as he intends it. These states are irritating sensations; unaffected disgust and acute repugnance; shocked moral, religious, or patriotic sensibilities; unsettling anger or irritation; and shameful embarrassment or invaded privacy.

Since the title of Feinberg's paper refers to offensive nuisances, it is worth noting that not all nuisances are offensive nor are all offensive things nuisances. Nuisances require one to make a small effort. Filling out university forms and the other petty administrative chores that faculty must perform are nuisances, but not necessarily offensive. Veterans of Foreign Wars selling poppies and "soldiers" of the Salvation Army soliciting contributions on the street may be nuisances but not offensive. On the other hand, garbage dumps, "dirty old men," and letters to the editor may be offensive but not nuisances. Offensiveness only creates a nuisance when one must make an effort to avoid it. Hence, Feinberg's requirement that offensive conduct not be easily avoidable limits the offense principle to prohibiting only that offensive conduct which is also a nuisance.

All Feinberg's categories of offense involve some form of shocked sensibility. He gives three sensibilities which may be shocked—moral, religious, and patriotic. To these may be added aesthetic and gustatory sensibilities as well as those of manners or decorum. Catsup on cottage cheese may well offend the sensibilities of even a non-gourmet. Public nudity, obscene billboards, and racially mixed couples may shock sensibilities of morals or decorum.[4] Displays of Nazi and Viet Cong emblems shock patriotic or political sensibilities, and desecrations of religious symbols shock religious sensibilities.

Since Feinberg allows shocked moral sensibilities as a form of offense, his offense principle gives a reason for limited enforcement of positive morality. It primarily differs from Lord Devlin's legal moralism by not providing a reason for prohibitions of private immorality. But it does give a reason for prohibiting public conduct contrary to positive morality. Feinberg's offense principle goes beyond legal moralism by also giving a reason for prohibiting conduct which is not immoral, e.g., "dirty old men" speaking to passers-by. Of course, all such conduct might be deemed immoral insofar as one ought not offend others. But that rule may only be one of good manners, not morals.

One may observe how much morality Feinberg enforces by comparing his prohibition of morally offensive conduct with Lord Devlin's principle of legal moralism. First, both require that the conduct be contrary to the fundamental moral beliefs of most persons in society. Feinberg requires the conduct to shock the sensibilities of almost any person taken at random from the society as a whole. Devlin requires the conduct to produce "intolerance, indignation, and disgust" in "the man in the Clapham omnibus," that is, "any twelve men or women drawn at random."[5] Second, Feinberg requires that witnessing the conduct be unavoidable and that alternative outlets be permitted. Devlin does not have such clear limits, but he does suggest that the maximum individual freedom consistent with the integrity of society be permitted and that privacy be respected.[6] A more liberal application of these conditions than Devlin seems inclined to make might well establish that people may privately engage in morally offensive conduct. One could simply claim that the values of liberty and privacy are not outweighed by harmless, private immoralities.[7]

It is important to be aware of the extent of the possible limitations on liberty which Feinberg's offense principle might justify. In a Mormon society, drinking tea or coffee in a public restaurant might be prohibited as shocking religious or moral sensibilities. In an excessively war-oriented society, a peace symbol or picture of a dove might be prohibited. Indeed, a hundred years ago a racially mixed couple could have been prohibited from strolling along streets in the United States. Further, it certainly justifies the laws against blasphemy in earlier days. These various prohibitions are possible because Feinberg only requires that conduct shock the sensibilities of accepted morality, religion, or politics. He places no restrictions upon the reasonableness of the objects of these sensibilities so long as almost everyone has them towards the same thing.

One crucial question is not faced in Feinberg's paper. He does not provide any general argument to show that protection from offense justifies overriding the presumption against criminal legislation. Such an argument needs to show that the evil of offensive conduct outweighs that involved in punishment. While it may be plausible that the evil of being offended is greater than that in a person's not being free to engage in offensive conduct, it is not nearly so plausible that it is greater than that in punishment.

Whether it is probably depends upon how many persons have to be punished, the severity of that punishment, and how many persons will actually be offended. In Feinberg's behalf one may assume that only light punishment will be given.[8] And the more offenders there are, the less likely it is that the conduct is universally offensive and so subject to proscription. Still, one wonders whether the evil of being offended, no matter what the cause of it, is greater than the evil of a few weeks in jail. To paraphrase Feinberg, it is hard to see how all offense is intrinsically evil (for example, that taken by a racist at the sight of a racially mixed couple); and even if one grants that it is, it has to be weighed against the solid intrinsic evil of the infliction of suffering.[9]

Nonetheless, Feinberg finds himself "driven, however reluctantly, to the offense principle." He justifies adopting the offense principle, not by a general argument, but by trying "to do justice to all of our particular intuitions in the most harmonious way." It is unsettled in moral philosophy whether arguments from examples can ever justify adopting normative principles.[10] Accounting for strong intuitions in particular cases is probably a necessary but not sufficient condition for adopting them. Hence, accounting for intuitions is a relevant but not conclusive consideration. Feinberg essentially has three types of cases which drive him to the offense principle: obscene billboards, speech abusive of minorities, and public nudity. These cases, however, do not necessarily drive one to the offense principle for it is not obvious that the offense principle accounts for our intuitions concerning them. In particular, the offense principle justifies too much.

Feinberg's discussion of the first two of these cases which involve freedom of speech or expression is curious, because he never brings into the discussion of these cases the generally recognized principle that restrictions on speech are harder to justify than restrictions on actions. Nor does he discuss the redeeming social value of the speech. He does make passing reference to these points in discussing Mill's views and prohibitions of obscene literature, but elsewhere they are forgotten. His brief definition of the obscene even omits reference to the dominant appeal of the material taken as a whole. Hence, all he leaves as a test of obscenity is that the material be "apt to offend virtually everyone." He does give a legal definition of "obscene" which is that it be obscene in the ordinary sense and not worthy of legal protection. But by the offense principle, there is a good reason for prohibiting everything which is obscene in the ordinary sense provided that it be unavoidable and an alternative mode of expression allowed. That is, the offense principle does not imply the usual legal tests of obscenity.

The results of Feinberg's failure to include the usual tests for obscenity are disastrous in the case of the billboard in Times Square promulgating the pleasures and techniques of homosexuality. Probably such a billboard would simply be lost in the sea of obscenity surrounding Times Square. In any case, Feinberg's principles cannot discriminate between a billboard which merely describes the pleasures and methods of homosexual relations suggesting that they are morally permissible (thematic obscenity) and one which in living color graphically portrays such relations. Of course, he derived the example from Schwartz who was commenting on the Model Penal Code and so assuming the usual tests of obscenity.[11] But Feinberg cannot make those assumptions unless he presents principles against legislation which justify them. Hence, on the basis of his argument, Feinberg has a good reason to prohibit such a billboard, contrary to present law, if it advocates sexual values which are offensive to the normal member of society.[12]

Feinberg's second case certainly works as much against as for the offense principle. It involves flaunting, abusive, or insulting conduct directed at subgroups of the population, especially racial, ethnic, and religious minority groups—for example, cross burnings, displays of Nazi emblems, and ethnic jokes. One may assume Feinberg only has in mind really vicious ethnic jokes, not simply Polish jokes. To do justice to his intuitions in these cases, Feinberg is led to an *ad hoc* abandonment of the universality restriction, i.e., that the conduct offend almost all normal members of society. He also appears to have abandoned the avoidability restriction for he wishes to ban such conduct from the public media. Surely such conduct presented via public media is as avoidable as movies and books. One need only check the television listings and have a rating system much as presently exists for movies. Further, if such conduct does occur, it has a legitimate place in news programs. If news programs can show large-scale killing in Vietnam, why not verbal attacks on minority groups? And there are borderline cases in which the implications of the offense principle are not clear, such as student protestors yelling "pig" at police and a Vice President referring to "fat Japs" and "Polacks." Such cases certainly cannot drive one to the offense principle. Indeed, Feinberg's offense principle simply does not provide a reason for prohibiting such conduct without dropping the key restrictions.

Finally, Feinberg's case of indecency involves a nude person entering a bus and sitting in the front. Such conduct will shock the sensibilities of morals or decorum of the other passengers. How universal this response will be depends, in part, upon how large a minority nudists compose in the population. Further, a large range of similar cases are already practical problems. Sticking to female nudity for the moment, one has the following cases: (1) being topless, (2) wearing a see-through blouse but no bra, (3) wearing a see-through blouse and a bra, and (4) wearing an opaque blouse without a bra. New York Penal Law has apparently set the standard that women may not appear in public without an opaque covering of the aurole and nipple unless in a play or other entertainment.[13] But if Californians accept the no-bra look and see-through blouses, Feinberg's offense principle does not support the New York law.

Borderline cases do not show the offense principle to be wrong or unworkable, but they do indicate its dependency upon cultural standards which constantly and rapidly change. Twenty years ago short-shorts, or "hot pants," were considered indecent by a large segment of the public. Indeed, they may still be illegal in New York City. Public nudity is an especially puzzling case because other cultures have accepted it, and it might be beneficial. It might help people overcome psychological neuroses about sex. There might even be other benefits. St. Augustine, for example, remarks that when his father saw him naked at the baths he noted his sexual development and found it a source of pride.[14] Ultimately, Feinberg's offense principle here rests upon the simple sociological fact discovered and enunciated by a lower Federal Court that "the American people are a clothed people."[15]

III

Instead of adopting a full-fledged offense principle and recognizing an interest in not being offended as worthy of legal consideration, one could take a much more cautious approach. Feinberg has defined harm as the violation of an interest. He excludes, however, one important interest, namely, that in not being offended. Such an analysis probably fits the ordinary conception of harm better than one which includes being offended as harmful. It is suggested, however, that rather than adopt the offense principle it might be preferable simply to expand the private harm principle, if need be, by admitting specific interests as worthy of consideration. Violations of these interests may be deemed "minor harms." The interest in not being offended may be divided into more specific interests depending upon the sensibility affronted and the object causing the offense. That is, one can specify interests in not having religious sensibilities offended by spitting on holy writings or sipping tea in a public restaurant. Each such interest can then be evaluated as providing a good reason for criminal legislation. Further, violations of such interests can be assigned greater or lesser weight for justifying legislation depending upon the importance of the interest involved.

This technique does not commit one in advance to the wholesale protection of the sensibilities of a large majority without examining the merits of the particular sensibilities and their objects. That is, one is not committed to protecting Americans from blasphemy just because they are a religious people. Further, one need not retain the universality restriction. After all, noncriminal legislation protects interests which only a minority have, e.g., poundage limitations upon tobacco production. Criminal legislation need not be restricted to protecting only those interests everyone has. Indeed, if one counts as part of criminal law the strict liability offenses in economic regulation, the criminal law frequently does protect rather specialized interests.

The crucial question, however, concerns the criteria by which sensibilities towards specific kinds of objects or conduct are to be evaluated. Essentially, if they are to provide a good reason for prohibiting conduct, they must be such as a reasonable man might have. The concept of a reasonable man may best be described in terms of what he is not. First, he is not mentally or physically abnormal. This condition does not exclude all who suffer from neuroses or physical disabilities, but it does exclude persons suffering from severe psychoses and, of course, neuroses or disabilities relevant to the subject at hand such as an abnormal reaction to church bells. Second, a reasonable man is not biased. One precaution which helps guarantee lack of bias is that he does not stand to gain or lose wealth, power, or prestige from the legal consideration of a particular sensibility. Third, he is not uninformed. He has all available knowledge about the conduct, its consequences, and the reasons for the sensibility being directed towards it. Fourth, he is not irrational. He can make deductive and inductive inferences. Further, he is influenced by evidence and reasons; they affect the attitudes and emotions he has. And he can defend his attitudes with cogent reasons. In short, a reasonable man is not mentally or physically abnormal, biased, uninformed, or irrational. Of course, reasonable men may have different sensibilities or direct them towards different objects.

Not even offense to the sensibilities of a reasonable man provides a good reason for prohibiting conduct. At least one of Feinberg's restrictions on the offense principle applies. One should require, it seems, that the offense not be reasonably avoidable. Hence, even if a reasonable man might be offended by pornographic movies shown in private, since the offense is reasonably avoidable, there is no good reason for prohibiting such showings. However, Feinberg's universality restriction should not be accepted. People may reasonably be offended by conduct which does not offend most of society. Many persons in society may be unreasonable with respect to that conduct. On the other hand, the fact that most people in society are offended by that conduct creates a strong presumption that the sensibility involved is reasonable. Of course, it may still be unreasonable; societies have had unreasonable sensibilities before. Nor does the provision of an alternative mode of expression for offensive behavior seem to make the offensiveness itself a better reason for prohibiting the conduct. Rather, this consideration more appropriately applies to the balancing of reasons for and against prohibiting conduct; that is, that a person is allowed an alternative form of conduct makes the prohibition less burdensome. Such laws are more regulative than prohibitive, e.g., closing hours in establishments serving alcoholic beverages.

So far the discussion has only concerned criteria for determining what forms of offense might be considered "minor harms" and so provide a good reason for prohibiting conduct which causes them. The difficult problems arise in Feinberg's hard cases. Attempting to reach a reasonable judgment about these cases involves considering good reasons both for and against specific legislation. Any conclusion is a personal judgment of the balance of factors. Hence, people may reasonably differ about particular hard cases.

Several of these hard cases involve, or may involve, freedom of speech. The presumption against criminal prohibition of speech is even stronger than that against criminal prohibition of other conduct because of the great value to society of freedom of speech. Thus, there is a strong presumption against prohibiting a wealthy homosexual's displaying a billboard if it is designed to carry, in a nonobscene way, the message that homosexual relations are morally permissible and satisfying. Against that presumption one may put the minor harm of people being offended by its thematic obscenity. But the moral sensibility which would be offended by such a billboard is of questionable reasonableness. Also, the homosexual is permitted alternative modes of proselytizing. Nonetheless, on balance such conduct seems permissible.

But suppose the homosexual displays a billboard that is obscene by the more or less usual constitutional test, that is, its dominant theme, taken as a whole, as judged by the average or normal person, appeals to a shameful and morbid interest in sex or excretion, and it is without redeeming social value. First, the presumption in favor of freedom of speech seems much weaker because the billboard is not as explicitly designed to carry a message. Also, it must be judged to be without redeeming social value. Second, the sensibility upon which the offensiveness rests seems much more reasonable than in the previous case. Third, an alternative outlet or mode of expression is permitted. Fourth, one must consider the effect of the billboard upon children. What may not be terribly disturbing to adults may be much more so to children. So, on balance, it would probably be justifiable to prohibit such a billboard. However, instead of simply making it a crime to erect such a billboard, one might merely have a statute requiring it to be taken down. Thus, the evil of punishment is avoided unless the owner persists in its display despite orders to remove it.

It is important to remember that there are other available forms of legal sanction besides punishment. The choice is not between punishing offensive conduct and doing nothing. It may be regulated, that is, restricted to certain times or places. In effect, allowing alternative modes of expression places much legislation against offensive conduct in this category. Of course, regulation is usually backed up by punishment for failure to comply with the regulation. But punishment need not be invoked immediately. People may be given an opportunity to comply after it is pointed out that their conduct violates a regulation. Also, compensation to those offended provides another possible sanction although its use may present many practical difficulties. Frequently, however, the minor harm involved in offensive conduct may only justify a lesser sanction than punishment.

The presumption in favor of freedom of speech also applies when minority groups are verbally insulted. Abusive attacks on minorities may well form part of speeches in favor of restrictive immigration policies and other social concerns. Offensive racial and ethnic jokes may be part of an entertainment program which really does entertain and amuse a large segment of the population. The Emmy-winning television program "All in the Family" rests on such material although some people claim that by insulting all minorities the program demonstrates the unreasonableness of prejudices. The abusive and insulting part of such speech may not have any social value or carry a message itself, but it may form part of speech which does. If so, then again the minor harm of offense does not appear to outweigh the presumption against criminal prohibitions of speech.

However, there are situations in which such speech may be prohibited. These are situations in which the context is not required for stating an opinion and the speaker has willfully and maliciously gone out of his way to insult and provoke others. Imagine a group of whites who surround a black on a sidewalk and verbally abuse him. Such conduct may be prohibited. Alternative contexts for expressing the opinion are available. And more harm is involved than offense to sentiments of respect and dignity. The black's interests in being let alone and not being involved in a fight are also violated or endangered.

Flag burnings, desecrations of religious symbols, and displays of offensive political symbols are borderline cases between conduct which is speech and that which is not. If such conduct is accepted as a form of symbolic speech, the presumption in favor of freedom of speech operates. Of course, it could still be prohibited in circumstances similar to those above, for example, raising a swastika in front of a synagogue as the members leave Temple. But the arguments for considering such conduct to be speech do not seem impressive. If it is not speech, then the special presumption does not operate. Further, the sensibilities offended may frequently be reasonable ones. Yet, the harm of the offensiveness does not seem to outweigh jail sentences. At most, fines would seem to be justified. And generally, people should be prepared for strong expressions of contrary political sentiments. So probably such conduct, at least if it affects only political sensibilities, should be permitted.

Feinberg's example of public nudity may be the hardest of the hard cases. Part of the vexatiousness of the case concerns the reasonableness of being offended by public nudity. Some reasonable men may not be offended by public nudity, yet it seems that others might well be. The reasonableness of the offense may depend upon the nature of the nudity, e.g., topless or completely nude. One must also consider what, if any, special considerations should be made to prevent children witnessing nudity. One may also reasonably claim that public nudity might provoke a breach of the peace. A year or so ago the appearance of an unusually buxom but fully clad young lady walking from the subway to her job created a large disturbance among staid Wall Street workers. In view of that instance, one can well imagine what might happen if a young lady, especially that one, appeared nude.

But to imprison a person for public nudity, if it was not deliberately designed to shock and alarm others (exhibitionism), seems to involve a greater evil than that caused by the offense. Perhaps the most reasonable solution would simply be a statute permitting officials to remove such persons from public places. As with the obscene billboard, only a persistent offender or one violating an authoritative order would be punished. Even then a substantial fine might be preferable to imprisonment. So although it may be justifiable to prohibit public nudity, one need not use punishment as a first resort.

Unfortunately, this brief discussion has not presented a clear, easily applicable principle. The search for such principles in hard cases seems a hopeless task. Such cases are hard simply because there is no obvious solution. Hence, it does not seem unwarranted to suggest that basic principles, like the offense principle, should not be accepted solely on the basis of a few hard cases. It is not as though without the offense principle one could not justify prohibitions of conduct universally condemned, e.g., murder. The position of a cautious expansion of the set of interests deserving various degrees of protection as minor harms under the private harm principle, while an uncomfortable position, has the merit of proceeding at a slow speed over rough terrain.

NOTES

1. The other liberty-limiting principles relevant to this paper are: (a) the public harm principle which prevents impairment of the operations of public institutions; (b) the offense principle which prevents offense to others; and (c) the principle of legal moralism which prevents immorality, especially that which is immoral by the standards of generally accepted or positive morality.

2. Herbert L. Packer, *The Limits of the Criminal Sanction* (Stanford, Cal.: Stanford University Press, 1968), p. 260.

3. See Michael D. Bayles, "Legal Principles, Rules and Standards," *Logique et Analyse* 14, nos. 53–54 (1971): 223–28, for a similar account of principles of adjudication.

4. Feinberg contends that public nudity produces shameful embarrassment or invades privacy. It is difficult to understand how the public nudity of others invades one's privacy or causes one embarrassment. Surely the privacy involved is the nude's, but one has not invaded it. For one to be ashamed of something, it must have a relation to oneself, be something for which one takes responsibility. One can be ashamed of the conduct of one's friends, for one may take vicarious responsibility for their conduct or consider oneself responsible for who one's friends are. Perhaps the shame and embarrassment one experiences at the sight of public nudity are due to one's emotional reactions to what one sees. However, it remains an open question how responsible others are for one's emotions.

5. Patrick Devlin, *The Enforcement of Morals* (London: Oxford University Press, 1965), pp. 17, 15.

6. *Ibid.*, pp. 16, 18.

7. Devlin himself does not favor prohibiting homosexual relations in private between consenting adults, but his reason is that it does not make him indignant and disgusted. "Encounter with Lord Devlin," *Listener* 71 (June 18, 1964): 980.

8. However, the Model Penal Code would permit imprisonment for up to one year for displaying an obscene billboard.

9. Cf. Feinberg, p. 95.

10.   See John Rawls, "Outline of a Decision Procedure for Ethics," *Philosophical Review* 66 (1957): 177–97; J. J. C. Smart, "The Methods of Ethics and the Methods of Science," *Journal of Philosophy* 62 (1965): 344–49.

11.   Louis B. Schwartz, "Morals Offenses and the Model Penal Code," *Columbia Law Review* 63 (1963): 681.

12.   See Harry Kalven, Jr., "The Metaphysics of the Law of Obscenity," in *1960: The Supreme Court Review*, ed. Philip B. Kurland (Chicago: University of Chicago Press, 1960), pp. 4, 29.

13.   Section 245.01.

14.   *The Confessions of St. Augustine*, tr. John K. Ryan (Garden City, N.Y.: Image Books, 1960), Book 2, Ch. 2, sec. 6, pp. 67–68. Alan Perreiah pointed out this passage to me.

15.   *Sunshine Book Company vs. Summerfield*, 128 F. Supp. 564, 569 (D.D.C. 1955); quoted in *The Obscenity Report* (New York: Stein and Day, 1970), p. 46, n. 14.

Reply

JOEL FEINBERG

Bayles' comments illuminate most of the matters they touch and advance the discussion to a higher level of clarity. Formulating adequate normative principles to govern the political control of private conduct, we both agree, can be construed as a task for a philosophical "ideal legislator." Bayles has my vote for that office, despite the minor disagreements that persist between us. Here I can only comment briefly on some of the issues he raises.

1. *The status of liberty-limiting principles.* Bayles' interpretation of various proposed grounds for justified state interference in private affairs is a definite improvement over my own, and I am grateful to him for it. Liberty-limiting principles are best understood as stating neither necessary nor sufficient conditions for justified coercion, but rather only specifications of the *kinds* of reasons that are always relevant or acceptable in support of proposed coercion even though in a given case they may not be conclusive. As defined in my article, these principles are not mutually exclusive, since it is possible to hold two or more of them at once, even all of them together. Hence, a liberty-limiting principle states considerations that are always good reasons for coercion, though neither exclusively nor, in every case, decisively good reasons.

This improved interpretation is especially welcome in that it protects my highly qualified "offense principle" from quick and facile counter-examples. Some critics (but not Bayles) have argued that my position would justify the prohibition of minor eccentricities of fashion or taste, for example, extremely long hair on men or crew cuts on women, provided only that they cause the most exiguous irritation to the overwhelming majority of onlookers. But all that my re-interpreted principle declares about these cases is that the fact of irritation is relevant to the question of the permissibility of the conduct in question, and relevant only if (or only because) it is nearly universal. Nevertheless, a relevant consideration can be outweighed by relevant reasons on the other side, and a merely exiguous irritation does not have much weight of its own. The necessity for balancing conflicting considerations is not peculiar to the offense principle. The harm principle, for example, does not justify state interference to prevent a tiny bit of inconsequential harm merely. The prevention of minor harm always counts in favor of proposals (say, in a legislature) to restrict liberty, but in a given instance it might not count *enough* to outweigh the general presumption against interference, or it might be outweighed by the prospect of practical difficulties of enforcement, excessive costs, forfeitures of privacy, and the like.

Moreover, when a legislature considers whether it should protect one set of private interests by interfering with still other private interests, obviously it must weigh those conflicting interests against one another to determine which are more "worthy" or "important" in general, and how heavily the general interests sit on the scale in cases of the kind under consideration. Like Herbert Packer, I hold that obscenity should be treated more as a nuisance than as a menace, and nuisance law, with its various tests for the balancing of interests, provides a model for how this might be done. (Indeed, nuisance law seems to be the model for the Supreme Court's *Roth* formula which Bayles chides me for neglecting.)

William L. Prosser, in his justly famous and philosophically rewarding text on the law of torts,[1] tells us that "nuisance" is a term with two distinct uses in the law: " 'Public nuisance' is a term applied to a miscellaneous group of minor criminal offenses . . . and 'private nuisance' is . . . applied to unreasonable interference with the interest of an individual in the use or enjoyment of land. . . . The reasonableness of the interference [Prosser continues] is determined by weighing the gravity of the harm to the plaintiff against the utility of the defendant's conduct."[2] So long as the interference is substantial and "such as would be offensive or incon-

venient to the normal person,"[3] the law will protect landowners
from it, provided it is not the unavoidable consequence of socially
important activities. But such interferences are not nuisances
where the annoyance is slight and the offending conduct reasonable.[4] Weighing the gravity of the "harm" to the plaintiff requires
the consideration of numerous factors: the extent and duration of
the interference and its precise character, the social value the plaintiff makes of his land, and the ease or difficulty of the means of
avoiding the harm are among them.

On the defendant's balance pan, still other factors must be
weighed:

> the utility of his conduct is always affected by the social value which
> the law attaches to its ultimate purpose. The world must have fac-
> tories, smelters, oil refineries, noisy machinery, and blasting even at
> the expense of some inconvenience to those in the vicinity, and the
> plaintiff may be required to accept and tolerate some not unreason-
> able discomfort for the general good. . . . On the other hand, a
> foul pond, or a vicious or noisy dog will have little if any social val-
> ue, and relatively slight annoyance from it may justify relief.[5]

Moreover, the defendant's conduct is unreasonable if it has a malicious or spiteful *motive*, or if alternative modes of conduct less
annoying to his neighbors are reasonably open to him. Finally,
Prosser concludes, "the interest of the community or the public at
large must also be thrown into the scale along with those of the
contending parties. . . ."[6]

It is not difficult to see how the interest-balancing model would
apply to the interracial couple in Mississippi. The interests of the
couple in free association and movement are of a kind considered
so fundamentally important to everyone that their protection is
commonly included in lists of inalienable human rights. The normal, spontaneous, joint comings and goings of the couple, free of
fear and anxiety, can plausibly be regarded by each of them as indispensable to a decent life. On the other side of the scale, there is
mere momentary repugnance in the eye of the casual beholder,
hardly as "weighty" a matter. Similarly, the state is ready to protect travelers on public buses or trains from severe offense or an-

noyance caused by the conduct of their fellow passengers, e.g. from shrill noises, overt sexual play, nudity, and so on; but the state will not prevent passengers from engaging in fatuous idle chatter in the presence of neighboring passengers, no matter how severe the annoyance, or the sheer boredom, induced in the unwilling auditor; for the interest in relaxed and spontaneous talk is deemed far more worthy of protection, on grounds both of private preference and public utility, than the interest in freedom from boredom. But that is not to say that the auditor's interest has no weight at all.

2. *Criminal and noncriminal prohibitions.* I also wish to acknowledge Bayles' important point that the criminal law is only one of numerous alternative devices for the control of undesirable conduct, and the one which carries the heaviest social costs. Some offensive conduct, no doubt, can be prevented more economically by reliance on individual suits for injunctions, or by court orders initiated by police to cease and desist on pain of penalty, or by licensing procedures that rely on administrative suspension of license as a sanction. These alternatives would not entirely dispose of the need for punishment as a back-up threat (or "sanction of last resort"), as Bayles admits, but punishment would not be inflicted for offending others so much as for defying authority by persisting in prohibited conduct. I doubt very much, however, whether all properly prohibitable offensive conduct could be controlled by such techniques. In some cases, we can know very well in advance that conduct of a certain kind will offend, that is, we don't have to wait for the particular circumstances to decide the question. Moreover, in some cases, there will not be time to get an injunction or an administrative hearing. By the time that sort of relief is forthcoming, the annoyance has come and gone, and the "harm," such as it is, has been done. In cases of that kind, the "interest-balancing" is done in advance by legislators, and the state issues a kind of blanket protection instead of a specific restraining order addressed to a specific person. In any case, I agree with Bayles that the penalty for merely offensive "harmless" conduct ought always to be less than that for conduct that threatens injury to individuals or harm to public institutions and practices.

3. *Offensive conduct and free speech*. Bayles regrets that I did not find time in my original paper to discuss more thoroughly the connection between the offense principle and the right of free speech. In particular, he criticizes me for failure to bring my brief early discussion of free expression to bear on the examples of obscene billboards and speech abusive of minorities. Let me try to remedy things here. I emphatically agree with Mill, Chafee, Meiklejohn, and Bayles that there is a greater presumption in favor of free expression than for freedoms of most other kinds, partly because the individual interest in free expression is so strong, and partly because unimpeded general discussion is vitally necessary to the general search for truth, which in turn is indispensably important to a myriad of public interests. I am so impressed by the case that Mill and other libertarians have made for the personal and social value of free expression that I would *never* permit the state to restrict or punish the expression of opinion[7] on the grounds of mere offensiveness. But it is crucial at this point in the discussion to make a distinction among the possible *sources* of offense in an offensive utterance. (Such a distinction will inevitably raise perplexities about the classification of difficult borderline cases, but, alas, that difficulty seems to attend most of the distinctions that lawyers and legislators must make.) One can be offended by the *opinion* expressed or implied by an utterance, as a devout Christian, for example, might be offended by the bare assertion of atheism, or one might be offended by something other than an expressed opinion, for example, an obscene poster of Jesus and Mary. The offending conduct might not involve the use of language at all; or it might be an utterance with no clear propositional content at all; or the expressed opinion might be only incidental to the cause of offense which is located in the manner and context of expression.

A recent Supreme Court case conveniently illustrates the distinction made above (and its difficulty). It was a hard case for the court because it involved the expression of political opinion in obscene language:

> WASHINGTON (Gannett News Service)—"Dissent by its nature involves the right to be offensive" said a lawyer, defending the public

use of "one of the most notorious four-letter words in the English language" before the U. S. Supreme Court.

A basic purpose of the U. S. Constitution's First Amendment (guaranteeing freedom of speech) is to protect offensive statements, argued attorney Melville B. Nimmer. His client, a California man, had been arrested for appearing in public wearing a jacket emblazoned with "F— The Draft."

The First Amendment, said Nimmer, protects the writings of Josef Stalin and Adolf Hitler, which are "more offensive than this word."

The appellant, Paul Robert Cohen, had worn the jacket in the corridor of the Los Angeles Municipal Court. Women and children were present.

Cohen was convicted of engaging in "tumultuous and offensive conduct" and sentenced to 30 days in county jail.

As the one-hour long argument opened Monday Chief Justice Warren E. Burger seemed to be implying that he'd just as soon the word itself weren't uttered in the courtroom: "The court is thoroughly familiar with the facts of the case and it will not be necessary for you to dwell on them," he said.

But Nimmer managed to utter the word—an Anglo-Saxon one meaning sexual intercourse—the one time it was spoken during the argument.

The court will probably rule on the case within a month or two. (*Mamaroneck Daily Times*, Feb. 23, 1971)

I will not venture an opinion about the constitutional issues in this case, but I can point out how Mill's kind of liberal principles, which I attempted to clarify in my article, would apply. Mill would argue that no political opinion whatever can rightly be banned merely on the ground that it is offensive. Thus one can shout to a crowd, or carry a sign or words on one's back, to the effect that we should abandon democracy for Nazism or Communism, that our troops should invade Thailand or bomb China, that sexual intercourse in public should be permitted, or that the Catholic Church should be nationalized—offensive as these opinions may be to many people. Similarly, one can condemn the draft and advocate its repeal, and do this in the imperative or exclamatory moods. But to forbid the public display of the sentence "Fuck the draft" is not to ban the expression of a political opinion because *it* (the opinion) is offensive; rather it is to ban the public use of a single word whose offensiveness, such as it is, has nothing to do with political opinion. If twins had appeared in the corridor of the Los Angeles Municipal Court, one wearing a jacket emblazoned with the single word "Fuck" and the other with the words "Down with the draft," only the former could rightly be banned on Mill's principles.[8]

It should be clear, then, how my qualified offense principle would handle "thematic obscenity." It would permit public *advocacy*, whether on billboards, or soap boxes, or in magazines, of *any* "values" whatever, pertaining to sex, religion, politics, or anything else; but it would not permit graphic portrayals on billboards of homosexual (or heterosexual) couplings. So precious is free speech on questions of public policy, however, that public *advocacy* of laws permitting graphically obscene billboards should be permitted. Indeed, public advocacy even of the legalization of homicide should be permitted provided the manner of advocacy itself is not offensive in one of the ways recognized by the qualified offense principle.

4. *My use of examples.* Bayles writes that there are "essentially three types of cases" which drive me, reluctantly, to the offense principle, namely, "obscene billboards, speech abusive of minorities, and public nudity." I did employ these examples prominently in my argument, but they are by no means the only kinds of examples I might have used. I might very well have discussed other examples of indecency and "flaunting and taunting," and examples of the other major categories of offense that I listed (irritating sensations, disgust and repugnance, shocked sensibilities) and still other categories not included in my miscellaneous and open-ended list of types of "offended mental states," e.g. acute boredom. So there was nothing "essential" in the examples that I did use. I selected them simply for their familiarity, vividness, and (I hoped) special persuasiveness.

I should like to take this opportunity to try one final example and to rest my case on it. It is an example that illustrates not just one but virtually all the categories of offensiveness mentioned in my article; and if the reader fails to concede that it provides a legitimate occasion for legal interference with a citizen's conduct on grounds other than harmfulness, then I must abandon my effort to convince him at all, at least by the use of examples. Consider then the man who walks down the main street of a town at mid-day. In the middle of a block in the central part of town, he stops, opens his briefcase, and pulls out a portable folding camp-toilet. In the prescribed manner, he attaches a plastic bag to its under side, sets it on the sidewalk, and proceeds to defecate in it, to the utter amazement and disgust of the passers-by. While he is thus relieving himself, he unfolds a large banner which reads "This is what I think of the Ruritanians" (substitute "Niggers," "Kikes," "Spics," "Dagos," "Polacks," or "Hunkies"). Another placard placed prominently next to him invites ladies to join him in some of the more bizarre sexual-excretory perversions mentioned in Kraft-Ebbing and includes a large-scale graphic painting of the conduct he solicits. For those who avert their eyes too quickly, he plays an obscene phonograph record on a small portable machine, and accompanies its raunchier parts with grotesquely lewd bodily motions. He concludes his public performance by tasting some of his own excrement, and after savouring it slowly and thoroughly in the manner of a true epicure, he consumes it. He then dresses, ties the plastic bag containing the rest of the excrement, places it carefully in his briefcase, and continues on his way.

Now I would not have the man in the example executed, or severely punished. I'm not sure I would want him punished at all, unless he defied authoritative orders to "move along" or to cease and desist in the future. But I would surely want the coercive arm of the state to protect passers-by (by the most economical and humane means) from being unwilling audiences for such performances. I assume in the example (I hope with some plausibility) that the offensive conduct causes no harm or injury either of a public or a private kind. After all, if the numerous tons of dog dung dropped every day on the streets of New York are no health hazard, then surely the fastidious use of a sanitary plastic bag cannot be seriously unhygienic.

5. *The problem of change*. Bayles is quite right again when he observes that the offense principle is dependent on "cultural standards that constantly and rapidly change." Even public defecation is common and inoffensive in many parts of the world, and there are many examples of conduct that was once universally offensive in our country but is now commonplace. I must grant these facts, but as a "reluctant" advocate of the offense principle, I needn't be embarrassed by them. One can imagine similar changes in the conditions for the application of the harm principle, but they don't weaken any one's confidence in that principle. Conduct which is banned at a given time because it spreads disease ought not to be banned at a subsequent time when that disease is rendered harmless by universal vaccination. Similarly, conduct which causes universal offense at a given time, ought not to be banned at a later time when many people no longer are offended, whatever the cause of the change. The two cases seem to me to be on precisely the same footing in this respect.

The fact of cultural change does cause me some embarrassment in another way, however. I now suspect that I was somewhat self-righteous in my criticism of Devlin's treatment of the analogous problem (for him) of moral change. Devlin might well have a *tu quoque* response to make to me. He could ask me a question precisely parallel to the one I asked him, and I would have to give an answer uncomfortably similar to the one he gave that I criticized as "uneconomical and ungenerous." How do the *sensibilities* of people (as opposed to their moral judgments) come to change? Surely one of the more common causes of such change is a steady increase in the number of offending cases. What once caused spontaneous horror, revulsion, shame, or wrath, as it becomes more common, becomes less horrifying and revolting. We become accustomed to it, and hardened against it, and then invulnerable to it, and finally (even) tolerant of it. But what of those offending persons who have the misfortune to engage in a given type of behavior during the transition period between the stage when the qualified offense principle clearly applies and the stage when it clearly no

longer can apply? Some of them, no doubt, will be punished for
what may be done a year later with impunity—and on my principle, rightly so. These unfortunate chaps are in a way like the last
soldiers to be killed in a war. They are treated no worse than those
of their predecessors in an earlier period who were punished in the
same way for the same thing, but their punishment, coming near
the end of an earlier stage of cultural history, is somehow more
poignant. To a later tolerant age, they will inevitably appear to be
martyrs punished for exercising their rightful liberties a trifle pre-
maturely. More to the point, their conduct had a direct causal influence on the attitudes and sensibilities they were punished for offending. Their punishment was for conduct that helped destroy the
very conditions that rendered that kind of conduct criminal in the
first place.

Thus, I am in the uncomfortable position of justifying the punishment of, say, anti-war demonstrators in 1965 for parading a Viet-
Cong flag (shocking!) while denouncing the punishment of other
protestors in 1970 for doing the same thing (yawn). Rapid cultural
change will always claim some victims in this way, and perhaps I
should sadly conclude that some unfair martyrdom in the transition-
al stages is simply inevitable, a tragic fact of life. My discomfort
in this position is at least mitigated by the thought that martyrs to
the cause of cultural change, on my view, should never be subject
to more than very minor penalties or coercive pressure. So the "trag-
edy" of their punishment is not at all that lamentable. Furthermore, "martyrs" of the offense principle are not as repressed as the
victims of legal moralism, for they are not deprived of the option
of engaging in the offensive behavior in private.

6. *Reasonable and unreasonable offense.* At several places in
his comments, Bayles points out that I do not require that universal taking of offense be *reasonable.* Providing only that the offense taken be *genuine* offense and that it be near universal, I allow
it substantial weight in legislative deliberations. Others have joined
Bayles in insisting that unreasonable offense should have no weight
whatever. Sometimes the argument for the latter position deploys

a hypothetical example against me. Suppose (fortunately contrary to fact) that the sight of an interracial couple *did* satisfy my qualifying conditions on the offense principle. Suppose, contrary to fact, that virtually everybody found such a sight intensely and profoundly offensive, and that such a reaction would equally be that of young and old, male and female, liberal and conservative, northerner and southerner, even white and black. Under those imaginary conditions, my principle might (subject to the reservations expressed in section 1, above) justify legal prohibition of the conduct in question, and that consequence is supposed to be embarrassing to me. This sort of example usually disturbs me for a moment until I fully grasp what the imagined circumstances would actually be like, and then invariably, the example begins to lose its intuitive persuasiveness. "What if . . . ," the question always begins: "What if something perfectly innocuous and inoffensive to any reasonable person, say, long hair, or white shirts, or eating chocolate candy in public, were to affect onlookers in some hypothetical society in precisely the way the public eating of excrement affects onlookers in our society?" In response, I am expected to recant and admit that there would be no justification, even in that imaginary community, for legal interference with the eccentric conduct. But as soon as I focus hard on the example and take it seriously on its own terms, it quickly loses all force. If the sight of a person eating chocolate affects all onlookers in that society in *precisely the same way* as the sight of a person eating excrement affects all onlookers in our society, then why should one want the hypothetical law to treat that hypothetical case any differently from the way in which the actual law treats the actual case? The example derives its initial plausibility from the difficulty of imagining that chocolate *could* be as revolting as excrement; but that difficulty, of course, is logically irrelevant.

I am resistant to Bayles' suggestion that I restrict the offense principle to cases of reasonable offense in part because so many of the forms of offense discussed in my article seem to have nothing to do with reasonableness. It is neither reasonable nor unreasonable but simply "nonreasonable" to be bothered by the sight of nude bodies, public defecation, disgusting "food," and the like. One can no more give "reasons" for these culturally determined reactions than one can for the offensiveness of "evil smells." Yet the offended states are real, predictable, unpleasant, and unmodifiable by argument; and these characteristics seem to me clearly to ground *prima facie* claims against the state for protection, claims that *can* be outweighed by stronger claims in the opposing balance pan, but which nevertheless do have some weight of their own.

Other offended states, I must concede, *are* subject to rational appraisal and criticism. It is perfectly reasonable to be offended by the word "nigger," and profoundly contrary to reason to be offended by the sight of an interracial couple. My principles would protect people, in certain circumstances, from reasonable offense, so that category raises no problem. As for most forms of *unreasonable* offense, the very unreasonableness of the reaction will tend to keep it from being sufficiently universal to warrant preventive coercion. As for the handful of remaining cases, there is still a claim for protection, it seems to me, even though offense is taken unreasonably. Providing that very real and intense offense is taken predictably by virtually everyone, and the offending conduct has hardly any countervailing personal or social value of its own, prohibition seems reasonable even where the protected interests themselves are not. Again, there may be parallel cases for the harm principle. We can at least imagine that because of some widespread superstitious (and thus "irrational") belief, virtually all persons in a given community react with such horror to a given type of otherwise innocent conduct that they suffer real physical damage, say to their hearts, whenever confronted with such conduct. Harm, of course, is a more serious thing than mere offense, but the point at issue applies in the same way to both harm and offense. The claim of superstitious people to protection from foreseeable harm is in no way weakened by the objective unreasonableness of their response to the offending conduct. Nor does the unreasonableness of the response count against the description of the resultant harm (heart attacks) *as* harm. The same points, I should think, would apply to foreseeable and universal offense when it too is the partial product of unreason.[9]

Perhaps the greatest source of my reluctance to restrict the offense principle to "reasonable offense," however, is that it would require agencies of the state to make official judgments of the reasonableness and unreasonableness of emotional states and sensibilities, in effect closing these questions to dissent and putting the stamp of state approval on answers to questions which, like issues of ideology and belief, should be left open to unimpeded discussion and practice. Much offense, for example, is caused by the obnoxious or aggressive expression of disrespect, scorn, or mockery of things that are loved, esteemed, or venerated. To take offense at expressed scorn for something that is not worthy of respect in the first place is, I suppose, to take offense unreasonably. But when is something truly worthy of love or respect or loyalty? To make *those* questions subject to administrative or judicial determination, I should think, would be dangerous and distinctly contrary to liberal principles.

NOTES

1. William L. Prosser, *The Law of Torts* (St. Paul: West Publishing Co., 1955).
2. *Ibid.*, p. 411.
3. *Ibid.*, p. 407.
4. "As it was said in an ancient case in regard to candle-making in a town, '*Le utility del chose excusera le noisemeness del stink*,'" *ibid.*, p. 399.
5. *Ibid.*
6. *Ibid.*, p. 413.
7. Offensive expression in art and literature is a more difficult and complex case impossible to argue here; but I would come to a similar conclusion.
8. I am forced to admit in this footnote that the United States Supreme Court did not follow my advice in this case. It overturned Cohen's conviction 4 to 3. (*Cohen v. California*, 403, U. S. 15 [1971]).
9. For whatever it is worth, I am cheered by the agreement with this

view of the law of nuisance from which I have derived so much stimulation. Prosser reports a case of private nuisance in which the defendant was a tuberculosis hospital and the plaintiff a home owner in the neighborhood. The plaintiff's suit was successful even though the fear of contagion which was the basis of the nuisance was judged by the court to be "unfounded." Virtually all the home owners in the neighborhood suffered from constant and intense anxiety that interfered with "the enjoyment of their land," and that very real anxiety constituted a nuisance, according to the court, even though unsupported by evidence of danger.

Law, Conscience, and Integrity

GERALD C. MacCALLUM, JR.

Here are some questions about law and conscience, formulated roughly for the sake of conciseness:

1. Does the law's demand for compliance sometimes violate or threaten to violate individual consciences?
2. Is the law's demand for compliance a contributing condition to the formation or survival of conscience?
3. Have the demands of conscience played a role in the genesis of and in determining the content of the law?
4. Can law or legal systems survive consistent deferral to the demands of individual consciences?
5. Can they survive consistent failure to defer?

These questions all seem worthy of attention. I attend here only to the first, asking not only for an answer to it, but also for an account of our stake in an answer to it. I contend that, given the way the issues are generally seen, the law's demand for compliance can neither violate nor threaten to violate a person's conscience. It can, however, lead a person to violate his own conscience in a way revealing to him his failure to live up to his own aspirations for himself. When we ask what stake we could possibly have in protecting people from finding themselves in such situations, we uncover a model of personal integrity underwriting the importance generally attached to giving conscience (some) priority over law, a model whose acceptability is open to serious questioning. I end by suggesting some grounds for that questioning.

I

Here are some ways into the problem of 'conflicts' between law and conscience.[1] The first runs variations on a simple story.

141

A little girl is playing on a railroad track, and a train is coming around the bend. A man walks by hurriedly, averting his face and quickening his pace; he is hastening to conclude a business deal of great importance to him. Though he remains ignorant of whether the girl was in fact slaughtered by the train, the incident lies heavily on his conscience for years after.

Another man is in the vicinity. He starts toward the girl to save her. But the embankment, made soggy by a recent rainstorm, gives way, plunging him helplessly into an icy river whose current sweeps him some distance downstream. The incident haunts him for years, but does it, *can* it, lie heavily on his conscience? If it does, he must regard his failure to reach the girl as resulting from some fault of his. Perhaps, contrary to fact, he feels that he could have kept himself from falling into the river if he had tried harder, or perhaps he comes to think that, being afraid of being himself slaughtered by the oncoming train, he may knowingly have chosen a route to the girl that reduced his chances of reaching her. We might regard this latter fanciful and try to talk him out of it.

A third man in the vicinity finds his way to the girl blocked by armed police. He too fails to reach the girl, and the incident haunts him for years after. Does it burden his conscience? We of course do not yet know; but how could it? The matter depends at least on whether he sees his failure as resulting from some fault of his. Naturally, the stories we can tell here are richer than in the previous case. Suppose he tried futilely to persuade the police to let him through or to save the girl themselves, and then tried furiously to break through the cordon. Suppose further that he senses no deficiencies whatever in his efforts in these regards—it was like trying to persuade a series of fence posts and like trying to fight his way through an impenetrable thicket; he simply could not do either. Could the incident, even so, lie on his conscience? The answer may depend on how he sees the police's being there and blocking the way so immovably and impenetrably, and whether he sees this as resulting in any way from any fault of his. Perhaps he feels in some way answerable for these features of the situation, feels both that he could have done something earlier to prevent them from being present and that, at that earlier time, he should have known and in some way really did know that something like this might occur—viz., that the operations of the legal system he supported, or at least did not subvert with all his strength, might someday make it impossible for him to do something he felt he must do.

These stories focus an understanding of "violate conscience" which allows that only something one does or fails to do can violate one's conscience, and that what violates one's conscience will, if it comes to pass, burden or trouble one's conscience. On this understanding, law could violate a person's conscience only if it were understood as something the person himself did, or, by extension, something resulting from what he did. This is one route into problems of law and conscience.

The major difficulty with this route is that it seems to miss what is on the minds of persons troubled about 'conflicts' between the two. These persons seem, at least in part, to treat law as though it were an alien and outside force impinging upon one in ways that may occasionally and seriously violate one's conscience. This view is most clearly expressed in the claim that it is wrong to force people to act in ways contrary to their consciences and that, in particular, it is wrong for the law to do this. A more marginal case of impingement of some sort is perhaps suggested when we are admonished, as we sometimes are, not to let the law become keeper of our consciences. Dealing adequately with the latter would make the present paper far too long, though the matter is touched on below. With respect to the former, however, I argue here that, insofar as such 'impingement' amounts or leads to violation of conscience, it does so by leading persons to violate their own consciences in ways revealing to them that they are indeed somewhat less admirable than they had hoped to be. The question we then face is that of what stake we have in protecting people from such confrontations with their own shortcomings.

II

Suppose that we start anew by attempting individually to view the law, as we are surely sometimes tempted to view it, as imposed upon us from 'outside' as implacably and unstoppably as the seasons of the year and, consequently, raise no questions whatever about the possibility that we have played some part in allowing this situation to occur or even in producing it. Seeing the law this way, we may also notice that its operation renders some activities utterly impossible (e.g., by bringing about death or incarceration or states of affairs such as that described above in the third of our cases about the girl on the track), but that its characteristic mode of prohibitory or compulsory operation is to render activities or omissions merely (though perhaps highly) dangerous or difficult or in some way unattractive or unrewarding. The borderline between these two main modes of operation is, of course, interesting, especially when one notices how nicely and conveniently it is obscured by the popular expression "out of the question," an expression likely to occur to us when the acts or omissions under consideration are likely to be followed shortly by our death, mutilation, or, even, incarceration. Postponing consideration of ramifications of that fact, suppose at present merely that the activities or omissions being (however) 'ruled out' are ones which would, absent the law, conform to the dictates of one's conscience.

The first thing to notice here is the importance of the expression "absent the law." There are two things to notice about it. It allows first for the fact that consideration of what the law directs enters into most people's understanding of what their consciences direct. Most of us think this reasonable enough, though the danger that it will be carried too far is precisely what leads some persons to admonish us not to let the law become keeper of our consciences. Obviously, however, not everyone carries it so far, and that is why we can have cases of conflict between law and conscience. This leads to a second reason for taking special note of the expression "absent the law," viz., the expression enables us, when considering whether the law *can* force anyone to act in a way contrary to his conscience, to take account of an important difference between the two main modes of prohibitory or compulsory operation of the law just sketched. I now turn to this matter.

Suppose, to repeat, that the activities or omissions being ruled
out by the law in the one way or the other are ones which would,
absent the law, conform to the dictates of one's conscience. Where
the law has rendered them utterly impossible—e.g., where its operation has led to incarceration of a sort making impossible repay-
ment of various debts, giving material help to the unfortunate,
actively seeking to end or imitigate the effects of certain evils, or
whatever else one might feel conscience-bound to do—has conscience *thereby* been violated? Well, in the first place, though the
circumstances may be highly regrettable, the person's present failure to do these things, seen as attributable to *him*, does not in itself
reveal a fault in him and thus cannot in itself reasonably be seen to
violate his conscience, though it is, of course, true that the circumstances leading to his incarceration may reveal faults in him, or that
faults may be revealed upon probing his role in creating the circumstances in which, the law aside, these acts of conscience from him
would now have been called for, or upon probing whether he now
believes these acts utterly impossible for him or whether he may
not have a 'secret gladness' that they are now impossible. Such considerations aside, his failure to perform the acts when they have
been rendered utterly impossible for him cannot reasonably be read
by him or anyone else as violating his conscience since it provides
no grounds whatever for reproaching him.

What, however, about the law whose operation made that failure certain? Can *it* be said to have violated his conscience? Given
our present hypothesis about the way the law is being viewed, it
could not have done so in a way that could burden his conscience,
for he in no wise sees himself responsible for it. Furthermore, it
could not have done so, at least within the confines of the present
description of the case, by so 'forcing' him to act contrary to his
conscience. This point, which might eventually need but will not
here get extensive argument, emerges when one considers that the
sphere of the actual operation of conscience is no wider than the
sphere of what is thought by the agent to be possible. Conscience
starts with what is thought possible. It can direct only what is

thought possible and reproach only for what is thought to have been possible; feelings to the contrary do not stem from it. Hence, rendering something utterly impossible for a person may or may not, if he recognizes the impossibility, change the character of what his conscience directs him to do, but it cannot *per se* put him in a position where he acts contrary to, or even in a position where he is prevented from acting in accord with, his (present) conscience. It thus cannot, at least in these popularly conceived ways, amount to a violation of his conscience.

The law, in short, does not and cannot violate a person's conscience by 'forcing' that person to act contrary to his conscience by making it utterly impossible for him to do otherwise. It cannot violate a person's conscience in this way because it is impossible for there to be anything corresponding to the description of the way.

The situation is dramatically otherwise, however, when one considers the other main mode of the law's prohibitory or compulsory operation, viz., rendering various activities and omissions not utterly impossible but merely dangerous, difficult, unattractive, or unrewarding. Here, most importantly, insofar as we recognize that the law has *not* rendered the activites and omissions *utterly* impossible, we can imagine someone resisting the law's 'demands' and, in the end, engaging in the activities or adhering to the omissions when doing so is what his conscience directs. Because we can imagine this, our consciences do not let us off scot free when the law 'forces' us in these ways to act contrary to them. We recognize that it was not utterly impossible (though perhaps 'out of the question') to do otherwise, *and that is why we can recognize that what has happened has been contrary to our consciences.*

If the law 'violates' consciences by 'forcing' persons to act contrary to their consciences, then it must be in such a fashion as this. But if this is so, then the following understanding of the situation is surely appropriate: if law here 'violates' a person's conscience, it is by leading him, through the obtrusion of certain considerations upon his consciousness, to violate his own conscience by acting contrary to it.

This understanding raises in a highly interesting way the question of what is at stake in the resolution of such 'conflicts' between law and conscience. It suggests that a person whose conscience is violated by his being 'forced' to do something contrary to it is always a person to whom some fault or reason for disappointment in himself or failure to live up to his highest aspirations for himself is revealed because he has so acted while realizing that it was not utterly impossible for him to do otherwise.

[The point is not always easy to see clearly, but I think it is sustainable. Imagine some variations on the situation of a man about to be drafted to kill people whom he believes innocent of any wrongdoing and also not in any way dangerous or harmful to mankind. The cost of his refusal may or may not be visited upon him alone. Certain hardships may also be visited upon his parents, his wife, his children. To imagine various escalations in these hardships is to imagine cases where it may become less and less clear to him that allowing himself to be drafted would amount to failure to live up to his highest aspirations for himself; but these escalations and the considerations accompanying them would also be making it less and less clear to him that allowing himself to be drafted would, in the end, *be* contrary to his conscience.]

Where, then, we have cases of persons 'forced' by the law to act contrary to their consciences, we also have persons confronted by a failure to live up to their highest aspirations for themselves. My question now is this: why should we think that these persons *merit* or *have a right to* protection against such a state of affairs, or, more softly, why should we want to protect them from being put in such a situation? Do we, for example, think it best or right that one never be put in a position where he is called upon and yet may well fail to live up to his highest aspirations for himself with regard to acting in accord with his conscience? Or do we think that occasions for it such as those produced by law are somehow gratuitous and avoidable? Or do we, perhaps, think merely that occasions for it such as these are regrettable and that we should do our best to see that they are minimized?

III

Full discussion of the issues raised by these questions would require specification of just what protective policies are being proposed in the name of the wrongness of 'forcing' people to act contrary to their consciences. Specific policies are seldom proposed in the literature on the topic. We might imagine them to involve advice or directives to police officers (don't arrest people acting contrary to law in order to avoid acting contrary to their consciences), or to prosecuting attorneys (don't prosecute such people), or judges or juries (don't convict them), judges or legislatures (exempt them from punishment, lighten their punishment, or somehow exclude them from the class of offenders), or merely the general public (respect them, don't 'condemn' them). Getting clear on such things is important if one is to come to grips with the fears of persons in whom talk of 'protecting' conscience against the law raises visions of immense and dangerous social confusion. But I am interested here in the prior question of what stake we have in giving any 'protection' at all.

Consider that on the one side we have (or can imagine) persons who, when we are prepared to admire them at all, we may recognize as having extraordinary courage and strength of character and maybe even heroic virtue, and who, if we are not at all prepared to admire them, we may think of as dangerous or harmful fanatics or perhaps only kooky fanatics[2]—persons in any case, who, no matter what the cost to them personally, resist the law's demands when the demands are contrary to their consciences and who, to make matters worse, may have unusually scrupulous consciences and thus be likely to confront the difficulty more often than ordinary men. On the other side we may have 'weaklings' who never, on such grounds at least, resist the law's demands when there is a conflict, though the extent to which the issue arises for them may be reduced if, as often seems supposed, their consciences are not so scrupulous. In between are more ordinary and perhaps also reasonably well-thought-of mortals. The first class will more than likely contain members whom we admire and might even wish, in our most inspired or fanatic moments, to emulate; but they are also per-

sons whose consciences are most noticeably *not* being violated by
the law's demands (unless we were to allow, and I think this would
be too much, that a person's conscience can be violated even though
he in the end acts in accord with it). Members of the second and
third classes (most of us) are by comparison, at least on present
grounds, less than fully admirable; they are persons who may very
well be led, in view of the law and the impingement of its operations upon them, to act contrary to their consciences. Commentators who say that one should not be forced to act contrary to his
conscience seem to have in mind the protection of these people,
and my question is why these definitively somewhat less than fully
admirable people merit or have a right to that protection. Precisely
what ends or interests would this protection serve and which (e.g.,
such as development of character or integrity) might it subvert?

In an age with a more deeply theological orientation toward conscience than our own, one of the stakes might surely be thought to
be salvation in the hereafter. Luther, for example, followed his best-
remembered words at the Diet of Worms with yet other words suggesting just this point. He said: "Here I stand, I can do no other.
It is not safe for a man to violate his conscience. God help me!"
But even here, though salvation may be at stake should the law
'force' a man to act contrary to his conscience, we may still ask
whether and under what conditions such a man would or should
be eligible for salvation.

In a secular age, with a secularized view of conscience, other considerations must be brought to the fore. What are they?

As a way of finding them, return for a moment to the cases of
'strong' men who, no matter what the cost, resist the law's demands.
Suppose we have such a person before us—a person who recognizes
that compliance with his conscience is an option for him though
difficult, dangerous, or in some other way unattractive to choose
because of how the law may or will then deal with him. Suppose he
resolves the issue in favor of conscience.

Shall we merely, or even at all, celebrate this as a triumph of the
human spirit? Or will we find upon close examination that there
has been much here to regret? Our answer will surely depend in

part on our attitude toward the acts or omissions that constituted compliance with his conscience on this occasion. If we think them undesirable or evil, we will, though perhaps admiring something about the person's strength of character, not in the end regret the fact that compliance with his conscience had been rendered so difficult for him. We may, indeed, regret that it hadn't been rendered more difficult, though this may be mixed with regrets that his conscience hadn't directed him differently, and with the realization that if this person had failed to act in accord with his conscience on this occasion even this might not have been a totally happy circumstance (more on this below). If, on the other hand, we think the acts or omissions constituting compliance with his conscience had been right or good in themselves, or harmless, or at worst 'inconvenient,' then we might regret the fact that compliance had been so difficult or dangerous for him.

But why should we? Clearly, where we strongly approve of the acts or omissions as right or productive of good, we may simply regret anything diminishing the chances of their occurring. And both here and where we find the acts or omissions merely harmless or at worst inconvenient, we may see the threatened punitive measures of the law as noxious subversions of the happiness and tranquillity of the person in question and as noxious costs placed on his exercise of free choice. But it is common to believe that more than merely these are involved when the acts or omissions are matters of conscience. It is common to see the punitive measures of the law in such cases as endangering the development or preservation of one's personal integrity and indeed of his status as a moral agent and even as a man—for it is characteristic of modern views taking conscience seriously that they place it at or near the core of a man's identity and tend to see subversion of his conscience as doing violence in a fundamental way to his integrity as a person, as subverting his status as a moral being and as a man.

Of course, any such threats were, by hypothesis, weathered successfully in the cases we are presently considering. Should this change our attitude toward them? Perhaps it should. Perhaps the effects of the experience were beneficial with respect to these very things; his integrity may have been strengthened (analogues: with respect to his rectitude in the face of external threats and blandishments—fire tempering steel; with respect to the coherence and unity of his personality—the unifying effects of polarization produced by perceptions of external threats), and his status as a moral being and as a man may have been enhanced. We might, on the other hand, think that the whole episode served only to reinforce a harmful fanaticism or rigidity of character. Or, even if we did not think this, we might nevertheless think that it was somehow gratuitous, that life itself throws up enough 'testing' and 'weathering' and 'tempering' experiences, and that the law's introduction of further ones is in some ways at best an uncalled-for redundancy.

When we come to the cases of persons for whom there has been nothing even approximating a triumph of the human spirit in such an episode—persons who end by acting in ways contrary to their consciences and submitting to the law—we will find some of these issues raised even more sharply. Again, our attitude toward the event will depend in part on our attitude toward the acts or omissions directed by conscience and those directed by law, whether we see them as right or beneficial and thus to be encouraged, wrong or harmful and thus to be discouraged, or neither of these and thus perhaps to be tolerated. These attitudes in turn will influence in one way or another whether we see the persons as of failed and less-than-heroic virtue, as fanatics happily coerced or persuaded into conformity, or merely as people whose inclinations toward nonconformity turned out to be not quite so strong as they may have thought. But, unlike the persons who in the end act in accord with conscience, these will all have reason for disappointment in themselves with respect to the incident. The incident exhibited a failed aspiration and perhaps one of central importance to them. Have they, in this defeat, suffered a harm from which they have or should have a right to be protected? What empirical and what moral hypotheses would underlie such a claim? And what models of human life would sustain it?

IV

The leading candidates for such harm are doubtless loss of self-respect and certain supposed consequences thereof. About these the following points may be made:

1. Whether a person suffers such a loss and the degree to which he suffers it depend in part upon what expectations and aspirations he has had for himself. Depending upon whether we find these latter disappointingly low, proper, unrealistic and destructively high, or simply wrong-headed, we may adopt significantly different attitudes toward his loss of self-respect and its consequences. (As an example of finding his expectations or aspirations for himself simply wrong-headed, we might find his conscience annoyingly, irritatingly, or even improperly scrupulous, as when we find him painstakingly scrupulous about matters that we find of no importance or in a way that seems to us to interfere with the satisfaction of more important interests of his.)

2. Whether, and to what extent, a person suffers a loss of self-respect depend also on where he places the present episode with respect to the seriousness of the offense against conscience and the severity of the penalties incurred or threatened were he to have acted in accord with conscience (cp. the difference that a white, integrationist pacificist might plausibly find between being required to ride in the front of a segregated bus and being required to do combat service as a bombardier, and the difference between thirty days in the stockade and a death penalty).

3. The extent of *the harm constituted or done to him* by the loss of self-respect depends on how he reads the magnitude of the loss. One can imagine readings on a scale sketched by the movement from "I am, alas, too human!" to "I am a cop-out, pure and simple," or "I am despicable!" It also depends on the longevity of the feeling (does it stick with him, persecute him, nag him, or does he 'adjust' to the situation by eventually, perhaps rather soon, turning a blind eye toward the episode?) and also on its consequences with respect to what sort of person it influences him to be and its influence on how he acts (does he pull down the flag of his aspira-

tions, or does he, in the course of time, do quite the opposite? And what *are* his new aspirations?)

4. The *wrong*, if any, we feel done to him may depend on whether we think it fitting or unfitting that he have such an experience given what he really is like.

These considerations raise an impressive array of empirical, conceptual, and moral issues. I cannot see how anyone can approach many of them with confidence. But our attachment of importance to them suggests a certain vision of what it is to be a man (and I say "man" advisedly, as you will see), and, quite apart from what may be the empirical conditions necessary or benign in producing such a man, and quite apart from whatever 'righteous' considerations might lead us to be or not to be tough-minded about confronting whether we are or are not such men, we might ask what the vision is and whether there is anything to it.

Important constituents of the vision are found clearly enough in Chapter III of Mill's *Liberty*, where he identifies, as distinctive endowments of human beings, the faculties of perception, judgment, discriminative feeling, mental activity, and moral preference, and says of them that they can be exercised and thus developed only by making choices on grounds conclusive to one's own judgment and "consentaneous to his feeling and character." One needs only to add to this something about the centrality of conscience in this integral and importantly autonomous individual—perhaps along the lines of Bishop Butler:

> Appetites, passions, affections, and the principle of reflection, considered merely as the several parts of our inward nature, do not at all give us an idea of the system or constitution of this nature, because the constitution is formed by somewhat not yet taken into consideration, namely, by the relations which these several parts have to each other; the chief of which is the authority of reflection or conscience. It is from considering the relations which the several appetites and passions in the inward frame have to each other, and, above all, the supremacy of reflection or conscience, that we get the idea of the system or constitution of human nature.[3] . . . in reality the very constitution of our nature requires that we bring our whole conduct before this superior faculty, wait its determination, enforce upon our-

selves its authority, and made it the business of our lives, as it is absolutely the whole business of a moral agent to conform ourselves to it.[4]

or of Arthur Garnett:

> . . . the conflict of conscience (moral approvals and disapprovals) with other desires (temptations) is not just an ordinary conflict of desires. It is a conflict in which the integrity of the personality is peculiarly involved. In an ordinary conflict of desires, in which there is no moral issue, the best solution is for one of the desires to be completely set aside and fade into oblivion without regrets. . . . But if the conflict be between "conscience" (the interests involved in moral approval and disapproval) and "temptation" (some opposed interest or desire) then it does matter which triumphs. The integrity of personality is involved. It tends to dissolve as a person slips into the habit of doing things he believes to be wrong. He loses his self-respect and his firmness of purpose.[5]

The constituents of the vision to which I wish to pay special attention are the autonomy requirement expressed so completely by Mill when he says that possession and development of those distinctive endowments of human beings depend on making choices on grounds conclusive to one's own judgment and consentaneous to one's own feeling and character, and the consonance-with-conscience requirement which both Butler and Garnett claim must be met if the parts of our inner natures are to be organized so as to satisfy our natures and, according to Garnett, preserve our self-respect and firmness of purpose.

One who accepts the vision with these constituents might indeed be anxious about cases where the law coerces people into acting contrary to their consciences. There is first the simple fact of action contrary to conscience—now to be seen as a threat to the benign organization of one's inner nature. There is second the seeming intrusion of considerations leading us to choose on grounds presumptively *not* consentaneous to our feeling and character.

But this last, of course, depends in the present context upon the first. It depends upon identifying something as dissonant with our feeling and character precisely on the grounds that that something is contrary to our conscience; the choice to comply with the law, made out of consideration of the baleful consequences of failing to do so, is to be thought dissonant with our feeling and character precisely because it is dissonant with our consciences.

One might give a quick and only slightly misplaced back of his hand to this suggestion by remarking that some people are cowards. Compliance with the law, contrary to conscience, is precisely in agreement with and suitable to the feeling and character of a coward. Etc.

If something has gone wrong in such a disposal of the problem, it has gone wrong because what is really a normative model of man has been taken for a descriptive model, though one of the strengths of the model is that if it is accepted widely and deeply enough as a *correct* normative account, it may more fittingly be treated as a descriptive account. That is to say, accepting it as a correct account of what ought to be the case will tend to give it a role as something to which one does in fact aspire or at least feels one ought to aspire, and a failure to measure up to it may then produce troubles of just the sort suggested by the model.

Should the model be accepted? It is the basis for common views on personal and moral integrity. It is highly individualistic and also, I believe, dominantly male-oriented. I end by suggesting how these are so and leave for some subsequent discussion whether they ought to be so.

It is highly individualistic in that the vision of personal integrity involved, a vision with inward-looking and outward-looking aspects, has as its rationale an interest in whether we have before us something sufficiently unified to count as a single person and sufficiently well-bounded to distinguish as one separable thing in an environment of other things.

As is made clear in the passages from Butler and Garnett, the person is viewed as a locus of various drives, impulses, needs, wants, thoughts, etc., but not as a mere assemblage of these. Rather, the person is seen as a locus of these so integrated with each other as to constitute a system of more or less harmoniously related 'parts.' In its inward-looking aspect, the person's integrity thus is seen to be a function of the extent to which his impulses, needs, wants, thoughts, etc. are harmoniously and 'coherently' integrated *vis-à-vis* one another. The rationale of this rests on an interest in whether the person is one "whole" or 'complete' thing rather than many things. The more harmoniously these 'inner' parts or aspects are related to one another, the more completely systematic the relations are seen to be and the easier it is for us to identify what we have here as a single thing rather than many things.

This side of the vision of the integrity of persons can of course be richly troubling. Consider how it is put by von Humboldt, quoted approvingly by Mill: "the end of man . . . is the highest and most harmonious development of his powers to a complete and consistent whole." Given the generally favorable attitude toward striving for and protecting the integrity of persons, this emphasis on completeness, consistency, and wholeness may be thought, for example, to enforce a disturbingly closed-off view of something so quicksilvery and open-ended as man sometimes seems to be. Plato might approve, but Walt Whitman would not. Consider Plato's criticism of certain actors in the *Republic* on the ground that "human nature is not two-fold or manifold, for one man plays one part only" (397e), and his criticism of the "democratic" man on the grounds that "his life is motley and manifold and an epitome of the lives of many" (561e); and contrast the following passage from George Kateb utilizing Whitman's view:

> Proteus could become the symbol of the tone of utopian life. The aim would be . . . to allow individuals to assume various "personae" without fear of social penalty . . . to strive to have each self be able to say, in the words of Walt Whitman's "Song of Myself": "I am large, I contain multitudes."[6]

And the matter has certainly disturbed Sartre and, less directly, John Dewey and other modern philosophers before and since. Sartre, for example, has been highly critical of people who long to be something "solid," something inescapable.

Of course, this so far neglects the central role given by Butler and Garnett to conscience in this inward-looking side of integrity, and the central position given that role may be all that preserves a plausible attractiveness for the view. It is true that we may have visions of being torn apart and thus destroyed by internal stresses produced by dissonances of desires and aspirations. But the valuing of *completeness, wholeness,* and *system* appears to go well beyond that consideration and to be attractive only if one sees them as in the service of "reflection or conscience" (to use Butler's nicely bridging phrase), i.e., as in the service of some model of rationality-*cum*-moral-stature.

Turning to the outward-looking side of the vision of integrity seeming to operate here, the side emerging when one presses on Mill's remarks about choosing on grounds conclusive to one's *own* judgment and consentaneous to one's *own* feeling and character, one can see this as underwriting the importance of the boundaries in the light of which we may determine what is a part of the 'system' of one's self and what is not. The self is seen as a bounded domain having an inertia or principle of organization and operation of its own and thus as one complete or whole and separable thing in an environment of other things. The upshot of attending to this side of the integrity of persons is that the integrity of a person or self is seen to be a function not only of the relations of his inner 'parts' or aspects to one another, but also a function of his relations to other things. Just as his integrity is seen to be increased with the harmony and coherence of the former, because he is thereby easier to see as one complete thing rather than many things, so his integrity is seen to be increased the more completely the state of his 'system' is determined by its own inertia or principle of operation, because he is thereby easier to identify as one distinct thing in an environment of other things. His integrity is *damaged* or *destroyed* when things within this domain of his 'self' become disorganized, incoherent, or unsystematic. His integrity is *violated* when the domain is intruded upon and changes are produced within it that interfere with and counter or 'overcome' the effects of his own inertia or principle of operation. And, of course, the violation of his integrity (outward view) may damage or destroy his integrity (inward view).

If the inertia or principle of operation of the system is identified, as by Mill in the passage quoted, merely with the person's judgment and with consentaneity with his "feeling and character," then the fact that a man out of fear or other aversion does something that is contrary to his conscience would not in itself amount to a violation of his integrity by whatever induced the fear or aversion. But if the inertia or principle is identified with "reflection or conscience," as it clearly is by Butler, then the state of affairs just described *would* count as a violation of his integrity because it would constitute a case of externally induced interference 'overcoming' the law of the inner domain.

The emphasis given here to the self as a *bounded* domain and the emphasis on consentaneity with the 'law' of that domain confront us, when they one way or another receive the approbation and encouragement generally offered in praise of integrity, with important features of what has sometimes been called "atomistic individualism." One need hardly do more than mention this last expression to raise a picture of the argumentative thrusts and counter-thrusts that might be delivered here when the whole idea is carefully considered.

My claim, then, is that advocacies of the special rights of conscience against law are based in important part in such foundations as have been exposed here, foundations which surely merit further investigation.

Touching, in closing, on the dominantly male-oriented vision of man that emerges when the above concept of integrity is explored, the orientation is revealed by the fact that deference—I mean *real* deference—of the sort that may not be consentaneous with one's feeling and character and yet is often though perhaps subtly expected from women, is notably not a constituent of the vision of integrity exposed here; that is, it is not a constituent unless one is willing to say that women on this account do indeed have natures different from those of men. The ramifications of one view or the other here are potentially of some interest. I hope to explore them on another occasion.

NOTES

1. I use double-quotes around expressions that are being directly quoted or mentioned. Single-quotes are used around expressions that are being used and not directly quoted but in need of having attention drawn to them because their use is, at least in the context, controversial or potentially at issue.

2. I am here of course allowing for the possibility of 'erroneous' conscience.

3. In *Five Sermons* (New York: Liberal Arts Press, 1950), p. 8.

4. *Ibid.*, p. 12.

5. In "Conscience and Conscientiousness," *Rice University Studies*, 51, No. 4 (1965), 76–77. Also in *Moral Concepts*, ed. Joel Feinberg (London: Oxford University Press, 1969).

6. In *Utopias and Utopian Thought*, ed. F. E. Manuel (Boston: Beacon Press, 1967), p. 256.

Comments: *My Conscience and Your Conduct*

HUGO ADAM BEDAU

I

In the opening section of his remarks, MacCallum implies that something cannot "lie heavily on" someone's conscience unless he regards it as wrong and regards himself as at fault for it. MacCallum also holds the view, stated later in the same section of his paper, that a law cannot violate someone's conscience unless the law requires him to do something, x, he does x, and doing x is wrong according to his conscience. These views about conscience and law are not, perhaps, wholly original; at least, MacCallum does not claim or imply that he thinks they are. I am more doubtful whether they are correct. Perhaps it will only emerge that I have not understood them. Let us see.

Consider an example. Through no fault of mine, you conceive a deep dislike for a neighborhood dog, and eventually you deliberately poison it. When I learn of what you have done, I am deeply offended, even though the dog is not mine, and it had no firm place in my affections. Because we are acquaintances, I bring up the subject in a conversation and, among other things, say to you, "What you did was outrageous; it offends all my principles. I want you to know that I enter my most sincere and conscientious protest against what you have done." "So you say," you reply coolly, "but 'sincere and conscientious' is redundant. Surely, what *I* did cannot do violence to *your* conscience. My offense, if any, cannot weigh heavily on your conscience; it cannot even trouble or disturb it at all." How should I reply to this? "You are right" seems to be what I should say if MacCallum's account is correct.

Yet to accept this correction is to dismiss the point I wanted to make against my neighbor. Since I know that I did not poison the dog, and that he did not poison the dog as a result of my advice or because he thought I wanted the dog poisoned, etc., and thus that I am not to be blamed nor at fault for the wrongful killing of the dog, my point in speaking as I did to my neighbor was not in any way to accuse myself for this wrong, but to express in part my judgment of him for it. That is what I meant to do when I spoke in terms of my "conscientious protest" of what he had done. Yet if MacCallum is correct I cannot use such words (or perhaps his claim is that they are not normally or properly used) in such a way. I am not convinced this is so. "Conscience" and its cognates have a place in the language of judgment other than the language of self-judgment—and not merely in the adverbial form as a synonym for "sincerely."

If it were true that (a) only the x that I do, cause, or authorize to be done, can make me guilty or at fault for an x, and (b) only what would make me guilty or at fault can be a violation of my conscience, then we could understand the restrictions that MacCallum and others place on whose conduct can be subject to the judgments of my conscience. But "violation of my conscience" in (b), like "conscientious protest" in my example earlier, is ambiguous. Both can have reference to something in no way limited to me, namely, my moral principles. "Violates my conscience" certainly can and sometimes does mean "violates my moral principles"; and a similar claim can be made for "conscientious protest." Since principles, insofar as they are moral principles, are very likely to be principles for your conduct as well as for mine, it is often incidental to judgments under them that the principles in question are clearly mine (but debatably yours), whereas the conduct in question is clearly yours (and indubitably not mine). In general, the answer to "Whose moral principles are these?" implies but is not implied by the answer to "Whose conduct are these principles for?" For these reasons, it is quite possible that though your acts are permitted by your principles (but perhaps only in conjunction with *your* view of the relevant facts), they are in violation of mine, and in this sense, violate my conscience and provoke my conscientious protest of them.

That MacCallum's argument ignores this point is clear from his remarks about the first of his three classes of persons discussed in Section III of his paper. When he says that their "consciences are most noticeably *not* being violated by the law's demands," we may be led to ignore the difference between the claim that by their actions in conformity to the law, they are not violating their consciences (which is true), and the claim that in the actions required by the law, their principles are not being violated (which is false).

II

MacCallum's central point toward the end of Section II of his paper (roughly, that a person with a violated conscience is a person thereby unable to live up to "his highest aspirations for himself") seems to me to be true. But as an explanation of why it is wrong for a person to violate his conscience, it seems to me to be incomplete. A further part of the explanation, I suggest, is that to do so is often to cause unjustifiable and inexcusable harm to others. When I violate my conscience, I not only typically disappoint myself by failing in my own eyes to be the man I wanted to be, I often also cause injury to others. I may be oblivious or inattentive to such injuries, but this in no way alters the fact that other-regarding reasons may also exist against my violating my conscience alongside those reasons of moral self-regard that MacCallum stresses.

For example, the soldier drafted despite his conscientious scruples not only diminishes his own stature as measured by the standard of his aspiration. He may also see himself, now that he is in uniform, as a danger to some of his fellow human beings, those his government designates as "the enemy," including harmless and innocent "enemy" civilians. (This, by the way, suggests why so-called "selective conscientious objection" deserves to be the vital moral issue it has become. Who can say for sure what is true about all possible wars and the rights and wrongs of his own participation in them when balanced against the harms of not participating? But many rightfully claim to be certain of the wrong and harm caused to the innocent by the Indochina war.) In fact, sometimes we might even endeavor to explain why the person who yields, despite his conscientious promptings, deserves to fall in his own esteem. It is because by failing to be true to his conscience that he has, through omission or commission, placed himself in the human chain that stretches out to harm innocent people. True, not all cases are like this. For example, the conscientious opponent of federal income taxation may not think that his refusal to pay his taxes does anyone (except himself) any harm. Still, the account of what we have in a person acting in violation of his conscience even in this case is too narrowly portrayed by MacCallum as of a person closeted with his own soul and caused to pass a verdict on himself on account of the gap between his personal aspirations and his actual conduct. The exclusive emphasis on this feature in the deliberations of a "man of conscience" will distort what we have before us by neglecting those aspects of what such a man does when he acts that directly affect the interests and rights of others.

In general, I might add that I do not believe that the best model for thinking about a person's struggle with his conscience is provided by a God-fearing Roman weighing whether to throw a pinch of incense on Caesar's altar. A better model (though, of course, we need not have only one) might be that of a loyal Athenian soldier weighing whether to carry out the decision of his superiors against the Melian colonists. Perhaps it is a misfortune for moral philosophy that whereas Thucydides records no such conscientious dissenter as I have imagined, history does record that many Christians and Jews died rather than yield to Roman practice.

III

Let me turn from criticism of MacCallum's analysis to sketch a general position rather different from his. Brevity will make my remarks more oracular than perhaps they should be, and I will leave it for MacCallum (and the reader) to draw out the consequences, if any, for his views.

I want to distinguish between *respecting* conscience and *appealing to* conscience; and I want to incorporate this distinction into a double thesis: (A) Whatever is of moral worth in respecting a person's conscience lies in the moral worth of respecting him as a person; and (B) whatever is of moral worth in a person's appeal to his own conscience lies in the moral worth of the principles espoused by that person. If (B) is true, then whatever is immoral about conduct in violation of a person's conscience can be restated without relevant loss in terms of the violation of his conscientiously espoused moral principles.

Some argument on behalf of (B) is needed, so I offer this as a start. Once a person has appealed to or invoked his moral principles (e.g., in rendering some moral judgment) there is nothing further for him to appeal to—of a morally relevant sort—under the rubric of "his conscience." Once my principles tell me that doing *x* is wrong, or that it is harmful to do *x*, or that doing *x* is contrary to duty, and therefore no one without very special counterbalancing reasons may do *x*, etc., there is nothing additional or contradictory thereto which I can bring forward by consulting or appealing to my conscience. For me to consult my principles *is* for me to consult my conscience. "I know what my principles require of me, but I wonder what my conscience has to say?" makes no sense. "Conscience forbids me to do *x*, but my principles nevertheless permit it," reports no intelligible dilemma. "Oh, to be a man of conscience and not merely a creature of principle!" expresses no meaningful lament. On behalf of these considerations, think of the following cases: (1) a person who doubts whether he has any moral principles but who is certain he has a conscience, and who therefore sets about trying to decide what morally he ought to do by appealing to his conscience; (2) a person who is certain that he has moral principles and certain of what they are, but who believes he has no conscience, and who therefore sets about trying to decide what morally he ought to do by appealing to his moral principles; (3) a person who has both moral principles and a conscience, but whose principles conflict or are at odds with his conscience, and who therefore sets about trying to decide what morally he ought to do by appeal-

ing in turns to his principles and then to his conscience. I think none
of these three cases can be seriously thought through except on the
most bizarre assumptions and with the help of the most fanciful
stories (or, worse, by exploiting trivial ambiguities in "principles,"
"moral," etc.). If they cannot be otherwise thought through, then
we cannot think through the difference between a person's having
moral principles and his having a conscience, and between a person's appealing to his moral principles and his appealing to his conscience.

If I am correct in what I have here asserted and sketched in argument, then all talk about the finality of my conscience for my conduct and about the consistency of my conscience's telling me not to
do x with your conscience's telling you to do x—all such talk is
suspect. Of course, if my principles are not your principles, then the
deliverances of my conscience will not produce agreement between
us in particular situations calling for moral judgment. But so long
as it is possible that your principles are true or right and mine false
or wrong, then my conscience is not final in any morally interesting
sense, nor are our differences consistent in any morally interesting
sense. The only good reason for holding a contrary view lies in the
fact that one of the moral principles which strongly commends itself to decent men is this: each of us should be allowed to act as his
own principles dictate—which is to say as his conscience dictates—
save only in extreme cases of immediate, irreversible, and indubitable harm to others. The danger in acknowledging "respect for
conscience" is that we will be led to esteem too highly the moral
worth of the conscience that is appealed to out of a due regard for
the moral worth of the person whose conscience is being appealed
to. Hopefully, the distinction I made initially in this section and the
resulting theses (A) and (B) may be of use in preventing that particular excess and the confusion on which it is founded.

Reply

GERALD C. MacCALLUM, JR.

1. When you poison a neighborhood dog, I may conscientiously protest. But it does not follow, even on Bedau's assumptions, that what you did violated my conscience. My protest may be 'conscientious' because I aspire to be a person who *cares* about what happens in the community and would feel myself falling short of this aspiration if I failed to call attention to the occurrence of the evil in question, failed to urge 'making it good' if that is possible, failed to try to minimize the chances of such occurrences in the future, or whatever. Thus, my protest may be conscientious not because what you did violated my conscience, but because my failure to protest when I had an opportunity to do so would violate my conscience. More generally, acts of yours that violate my moral principles may draw my 'conscientious' protest because not only do I believe that you as well as I ought to act in accord with the principles in question, but I aspire to take or to feel myself responsible for taking measures to see that others as well as myself act in accord with the principles and would feel remiss if I failed to take those measures. (Two caveats about this: The nature of the connection between having the aspiration or the feeling of responsibility in question and having the moral principles is worth exploring but too complex to take up here; and which question about 'measures' one takes or contemplates taking, and in which cases, are important —we tend to admire persons who 'care' about what happens in the world and who act out their caring, but we are also capable of criticizing people for being moral busybodies and for attempting to be world cops.) A rich supply of alternative accounts equally consistent with my thesis becomes available if one is permitted to alter one small feature of Bedau's description of the case, viz., that I

'know' that I am not to be blamed or at fault for the wrongful killing of the dog. As my remarks on variations two and three of the
story in Part I of my essay suggest, people exhibit an interesting
capacity to grow unclear about such matters when they think of
them.

2. Bedau and I appear to me to be largely in agreement on the
issues he raises in Parts II and III of his commentary. Compare the
fourth-to-last, third-to-last, and last paragraphs of Part III of my
essay. These paragraphs exhibit the agreement and make clear that
my emphasis is different because I am after different game.

3. Bedau's remarks about the connection between conscience
and principles are interesting but, I believe, best suited to clearly
'secularized' conscience and thus perhaps best stated less generally
than he states them.

Selected Bibliography

What follows is a short list of materials relevant in different ways to questions about the justification of violations of established principles and rules, or common human attitudes and sentiments, of social life. Nearly all the materials are recent or contemporary and hence do not include such classics as Plato's *Crito* or the literature associated historically with the social-contract theory of political obligation. The notes accompanying many of the contributions to the symposia published in this volume provide further suggestions for study.

Bedau, Hugo Adam, ed. *Civil Disobedience: Theory and Practice.* New York: Pegasus, 1969.
Benn, S. I. and R. S. Peters. *The Principles of Political Thought.* New York: The Free Press, 1959. (Original title: *Social Principles and the Democratic State* [London: George Allen and Unwin Ltd., 1959].)
Cohen, Marshall. "Civil Disobedience in a Constitutional Democracy," *Massachusetts Review* 10 (Summer, 1969): 211–26.
Devlin, Patrick. *The Enforcement of Morals.* London: Oxford University Press, 1965.
Dworkin, Ronald. "Lord Devlin and the Enforcement of Morals," *Yale Law Journal* 75 (1966): 986–1005. "On Not Prosecuting Civil Disobedience," *The New York Review of Books* 10 (June 6, 1968): 14–21. "Taking Rights Seriously," *The New York Review of Books* 15 (December 17, 1970), 23–31. "Philosophy and the Critique of Law," in *Society: Revolution and Reform*, edited by Robert H. Grimm and Alfred F. MacKay (Cleveland and London: The Press of Case Western Reserve University, 1971), pp. 59–81, together with comments by Gerald C. MacCallum Jr.
Finn, James, ed. *A Conflict of Loyalties: The Case for Selective Conscientious Objection.* New York: Pegasus, 1968.

Friedrich, Carl J., ed. *Nomos VIII: Revolution.* New York: Atherton, 1966.

Fuller, Lon L. "Positivism and Fidelity to Law—A Reply to Professor Hart," *Harvard Law Review* 71 (1958): 630–72. A response to H. L. A. Hart's "Positivism and the Separation of Law and Morals" (see Hart, below); reprinted in *Society, Law, and Morality*, edited by Frederick A. Olafson (Englewood Cliffs, N.J.: Prentice-Hall, Inc., 1961), pp. 471–505.

Garnett, A. Campbell. "Conscience and Conscientiousness." In *Rice University Studies* 51 (No. 4) (1965): 71–83. Reprinted in *Moral Concepts*, edited by Joel Feinberg. London: Oxford University Press, 1970, 80–92.

Gewirth, Alan. "Civil Disobedience, Law, and Morality: An Examination of Justice Fortas' Doctrine," *The Monist* 54 (1970): 536–55. "Obligation: Political, Legal, Moral," in *Nomos XII: Political and Legal Obligations*, edited by J. Roland Pennock and John W. Chapman (New York: Atherton, 1970), pp. 55–88.

Grimm, Robert H., and Alfred F. MacKay, eds. *Society: Revolution and Reform.* Cleveland and London: The Press of Case Western Reserve University, 1971. The proceedings of the 1969 Oberlin Colloquium in Philosophy.

Hart, H. L. A. "Positivism and the Separation of Law and Morals," *Harvard Law Review* 71 (1958): 593–629. Reprinted in *Society, Law, and Morality*, edited by Frederick A. Olafson (Englewood Cliffs, N.J.: Prentice-Hall, Inc., 1961), 439–70 (see Fuller's response listed above). *Law, Liberty, and Morality*. London: Oxford University Press, 1963.

Held, Virginia, Kai Nielsen, and Charles Parsons, eds. *Philosophy and Political Action.* London: Oxford University Press, 1972.

Kaufman, Arnold S. *The Radical Liberal.* New York: Atherton, 1968. "Democracy and Disorder," in *Society: Revolution and Reform*, edited by Robert H. Grimm and Alfred F. MacKay (Cleveland and London: The Press of Case Western Reserve University, 1971), pp. 33–52, together with comments by Felix E. Oppenheim.

MacCallum, Gerald C., Jr. "Negative and Positive Freedom," *Philosophical Review* 76 (1967): 312–34.

Mayer, Peter, ed. *The Pacifist Conscience*. New York: Holt, Rinehart and Winston, 1966.

Miliband, Ralph. *The State in Capitalist Society*. London: Weidenfeld and Nicolson, 1969.

Mill, John Stuart. *On Liberty* (1859). See also Mill's *Utilitarianism* (1863), esp. Ch. III.

Rawls, John. *A Theory of Justice* (Cambridge, Mass.: Harvard University Press, 1971). Important papers published prior to *A Theory of Justice* are "Justice as Fairness," *Philosophical Review* 67 (1958): 164–94, reprinted (slightly revised) in *Philosophy, Politics, and Society*, Second Series, edited by Peter Laslett and W. G. Runciman (Oxford: Blackwell, 1962), pp. 132–57; "Constitutional Liberty and the Concept of Justice," in *Nomos VI: Justice*, edited by Carl J. Friedrich and John W. Chapman (New York: Atherton, 1963), pp. 98–125; "The Sense of Justice," *Philosophical Review* 72 (1963): 281–305, reprinted in *Moral Concepts*, edited by Joel Feinberg (London: Oxford University Press, 1970), pp. 120–40; "Distributive Justice," in *Philosophy, Politics, and Society*, Third Series, edited by Peter Laslett and W. G. Runciman, (Oxford: Blackwell, 1967), pp. 58–82; "The Justification of Civil Disobedience," in *Civil Disobedience: Theory and Practice*, edited by Hugo Adam Bedau (see above).

Runciman, W. G. *Relative Deprivation and Social Justice*. London: Routledge and Kegan Paul, 1966.

Shaffer, Jerome A., ed. *Violence*. New York: David McKay Company, 1971. A collection of award-winning essays from a competition sponsored by the Council for Philosophical Studies, together with a selected bibliography.

Vlastos, Gregory. "Justice and Equality," in *Social Justice*. Edited by Richard B. Brandt. Englewood Cliffs, N.J.: Prentice-Hall, Inc., 1962, 31–72. Partially reprinted as "Human Worth, Merit, and Equality," in *Moral Concepts*. Edited by Joel Feinberg. London: Oxford University Press, 1970, pp. 141–52.

Walzer, Michael. *Obligations*. Cambridge, Mass.: Harvard University Press, 1970.

Wasserstrom, Richard A. "The Obligation to Obey the Law," *U.C.L.A. Law Review* 10 (1963): 780–810, reprinted in *Essays in Legal Philosophy*, edited by Robert S. Summers (Oxford: Blackwell, 1968), pp. 274–304. "Rights, Human Rights, and Racial Discrimination," *Journal of Philosophy* 61 (1964): 628–41. "On the Morality of War: A Preliminary Inquiry," *Stanford Law Review* 21 (1969): 1627–56.

Williams, Bernard. "The Idea of Equality," in *Philosophy, Politics, and Society*, Second Series. Edited by Peter Laslett and W. G. Runciman. Oxford: Blackwell, 1962, pp. 110–31.

Wolff, Robert Paul. "On Violence," *Journal of Philosophy* 66 (1969): 601–16. *In Defense of Anarchism*. New York: Harper and Row, 1970.